Spiritual Violence

Religious Phenomena that Defile the Faith

SPIRITUAL VIOLENCE

RELIGIOUS PHENOMENA THAT DEFILE THE FAITH

Rev. Alba Onofrio

with Nadia Arellano
and Dr. Judith Bautista Fajardo

Soulforce Inc.

Spiritual Violence: Religious Phenomena that Defile the Faith

Adapted from ***Violencia Espiritual y fenómenos religiosos que abusan de la fe***

www.soulforce.org

Published for Soulforce, Inc.

Authors — Rev. Alba Onofrio, Nadia Arellano, & Dr. Judith Bautista Fajardo
Editor — Dr. Aly Benítez
Illustrations and design — Bryony Dick

ISBN: 978-1-7361267-8-3

Dedication

As long as there has been empire,
there have been those of us who resist it.

In brazen defiance of white Christian Supremacy and
with deepest devotion to our faith and our people,
we offer this book as an attempt
to break the silence around the embedded power structures
in our churches and societies.

To all our hermanxs Sinvergüenzas:

You, who came before us, thank you
for lending us strength and wisdom.

You, who are with us now, thank you
for making us courageous as we walk
through the valley of the shadow of death.

You, who are to come, thank you
for offering us the hope of resurrection.

Todxs, PRESENTE!

Acknowledgements

This book is the result of communal labor, theological struggle, and shared commitments to truth-telling and healing within Christian traditions. I am grateful to all who contributed to the first volume and Spanish edition. The process of ideating content, collecting testimonies, writing, and editing by the team of Karina Vargas, Judith Bautista Fajardo, Aly Benítez, and myself co-created that edition and laid the foundation for this work.

I offer special thanks to **Karina Vargas**, whose leadership and authorship were central to the original project. Our collaboration—emerging from her lived experience of Religious Abuse and Spiritual Trauma and my work on Spiritual Violence and white Christian Supremacy—shaped the theological and pastoral commitments of this book from its inception in 2021. Though this English edition has been substantially revised for use in educational settings, the content for the Reflective Awareness Tools and healing strategies captured in the appendices remain deeply indebted to her work.

Equally formative are the somatic practices authored by **Dr. Judith Bautista Fajardo**, preserved here in translation. These practices invite readers into embodied forms of discernment and care, particularly for Queer and Trans communities whose bodies have too often been sites of theological harm.

This work was also sustained by the collective care and leadership of the **Soulforce staff,** whose generosity made its completion possible. I could not have imagined a more dedicated or committed team. Within that community, I want to name **Nadia Arellano,** whose lived experience and rigorous engagement with research made the chapter on Spiritual Trauma more robust and grounded in lived reality.

The interdisciplinary depth of this book was further strengthened through the thoughtful engagement of **Dr. Norma Ramírez Miranda, Dr. Alicia Trotman,** and **Dr. Sahnya Thom,** who offered psychological and clinical perspectives that sharpened its approach to trauma, healing, and pastoral care. Their contributions help ensure that the material is both ethically grounded and practically useful for students, educators, and practitioners. I offer particular thanks to **Dr. Sahnya Thom** for her ongoing leadership in developing a psychometrically validated instrument based on the Reflective Awareness Tools. This work brings needed rigor and care to the assessment of spiritual harm and deepens this book's contribution at the intersection of theology, psychology, and pastoral formation.

Creative and sustaining support also shaped this project in essential ways. My thanks extend to **Bryony Dick,** whose artistic vision renders complex ideas accessible and alive, and to **Dr. Aly Benítez,** whose care, encouragement, and editorial support carried me through every stage of this work.

At its core, this book is grounded in the courage of **survivors** who entrusted us with their stories. Their vulnerability makes it possible to engage Spiritual Violence not as an abstract concept, but as a lived ethical crisis of faith—one that demands faithful, informed response from students, educators, clergy, and communities alike. My deepest gratitude to this community.

Table of Contents

Sinvergüenza

feminine adjective · common noun

One who acts or speaks without restraint. sassy. rude. irreverent.
Behaves in ways that own her sexuality without shame.
Commits illicit acts for one's own benefit.
Impertinent. bold. audacious.

Prologue

Lxs Sinvergüenzas was born as an act of faithful resistance within a courageous communal process of spiritual self-reclamation that moves us away from the fear of being labeled a *sinvergüenza*—one who is "too loud," "too sexual," "too opinionated," "too colorful," "too political," "too queer"—a femininity that is just too much all around. As Sinvergüenzas, we move towards a sense of self-possession and pride in openly being our authentic selves and raising our voices without shame.

As people of faith and theologians, we commit ourselves politically as Queer and feminist. As Queer feminists, we affirm our deep and abiding faith. We are activists, healers, parents and grandparents, faith leaders, scholars, artists, students, and more. Not all of us identify with all the labels: Latinoamericana/ Latinx, Christian, Queer, feminist, but we find community together in the *sinvergüenza*—a reclaimed word originally used to reprimand, insult, silence, and demean. We cross borders and work collaboratively to bridge difference and center our shared humanity.

We affirm that Latinx is not a static monolithic identity; we come from an incredible diversity of languages, geographies, races and cultures. Our migration narratives, survival strategies, and current contextual realities are as creative and varied as our origin stories. The question of "Latinidad" as a unifying identity marker for those with Latin American roots who live in diaspora is still very much up for debate with sharp critiques about its embedded anti-Black racism and indigenous erasure. While many continue to identify with their specific home country, race, and/or indigenous community, I use the term here to signal some of the ways in which the colonizer made us kin, of sorts, and how white Christian Supremacy hopefully makes us co-conspirators in its demise and our communities' healing.

As a methodological approach to theology, Teología Sin Vergüenza grows out of an ethic of solidarity that centers the experiences of those directly affected by religion-based violence throughout Latin America and its diaspora. We have adapted the content here for a US, English-speaking audience, because we honor the reality that not all of us whose roots were grown in the earth of *Abya Yala*[1] speak Spanish or have direct access to the robust activist and feminist theological communities fighting and loving across what is now called Latin America and the Spanish-speaking Caribbean.

Nevertheless, it is our right to learn from these legacies of faithful resistance, even as we live in diaspora. This book is especially intended for the Sinvergüenzas who feel that we are *ni de aquí, ni de allá*[2] but carry the wounds of physical and spiritual displacement wherever we go.

This text was first conceptualized as a transnational collaborative project between the digital media project, Teología Sin Vergüenza, and the international LGBTQIA+ nonprofit, Soulforce. The original book project, ***Violencia Espiritual y fenómenos religiosos***

que abusan de la fe was co-written in Spanish by Karina Vargas, Judith Bautista Fajardo, and myself, and edited by Aly Benítez and Nadia Arellano as a foundational text for the Institute on Spiritual Violence, Healing, and Social Change. It was conceived for and by Queer and feminist women who also fold in our work as theologians, activists, survivors, faith leaders, somatic healers, and/or mental health professionals. While the original plan was to simply translate the book into English, that proved to be naïve. Cultural references, histories of colonization, and linguistic idiosyncrasies made a straightforward translation impossible. In this US-English adaptation of this work, I take personal responsibility for content choices; the use of first-person is my own *autohistoria-teoría* referencing my personal feelings, beliefs, and experiences over the last twenty years in social justice movements and LGBTQIA+ community.

Introduction

As we visit with feminist and LGBTQIA+ communities around the world, there is this sacred moment in which my heart shatters to pieces.[3] In the hushed tones of a confession, the person before me reveals that they still love God… just quietly now and in private. Their faith is expressed in the small rituals of daily life and in their silent pleas for help in times of crisis. They have not, in fact, abandoned their faith, though in many very real ways, it seems as though God and those who claim to be God's people, have abandoned them. In those intimate pastoral encounters, my soul catches fire again, hot with the righteous indignation of spiritual injustice. It is only love, fueled by rage, that can burn hot enough to meld the broken shards back together into something the shape of my heart.

The horror stories of conversion therapy, the excommunication from families and churches, the struggle to stay alive—these are all familiar narratives by now. I'm no longer shocked to receive them. From genital mutilation to imprisonment, to electroshock therapy to forced marriage and "corrective" rape—physical, psychological and emotional violence are a centerpiece of everyday life. Fear, shame, and grief are constant bedfellows. The experiences are slightly different in the nuances of culture and political context and church denomination, but the traumas are remarkably similar, each devastating in their own ways, forever changing the lives of those who survive them, and forever marking the communities of those who don't.

It is easy to recoil or shake our heads disapprovingly. We offer our heartfelt thoughts and prayers and talk in cliches about how "God is Love" and "Love Wins." Some of us can even offer discouraging statistics on public health outcomes for our community or the latest political attack on our rights. But what is not being talked about is the Spiritual Violence that comes from the underlying Christian ideological foundation that legitimizes and even demands punitive action against anyone who does not conform to the rigid constructs of gender and sexuality—what we refer to as white Christian Supremacy.[4]

Despite the violence, many of us still carry deep-rooted attachments to the Divine within us, even when we can no longer maintain the membership requirements for acceptance in a religious family or faith community. We cling to practices and beliefs that help us feel connected to our faith, even if we must flee the very families and institutions who instilled Christianity in us. Some decide to reject faith altogether; others convert to a different religion, and many of us expand our spiritualities to make them more inclusive and representative of who we are becoming. Regardless of where we land religiously, almost all of us carry the wounds of Spiritual Violence: shame, guilt, and fear of being judged, found unworthy of love, and condemned to eternal suffering. These remain in the silent recesses of our being, lingering long after our rational minds have explained them away.

Because our religious beliefs and faith practices are so connected to the marrow of who we are as people—carrying our cultures and foodways, family histories, and personal beliefs—it is often elevated to an untouchable status. Particularly in the United States, where our nation's origin story begins with Christian immigrants persecuted and seeking freedom in a new land to practice their faith, most people go along with the discourse of Christian religious liberty no matter how extreme the rhetoric or the violence that follows. However, those wielding this language are almost never marginalized minority communities; it is almost exclusively leveraged in the public sphere to refuse services to LGBTQIA+ people or to deny reproductive healthcare to people seeking abortions.

Christianity, as far as it colludes with systems of power, must be contested. Regardless of personal spirituality, religion affects every aspect of our lives because Christianity is the religion of power on our continent. It is the origin of our ideas of right and wrong and the basis for everything from our society's legal system to cultural beauty standards to ideals for home and family. Especially for Christians, it is our inheritance and responsibility to address the ways in which our religion is used for violence in all its forms. Despite the taboo surrounding it, it's critical that we start talking about religion-based violence based in white Christian Supremacy.

Envisioned and framed in transnational activist spaces, this work focuses on the parasitic relationship between religion and power that produces white Christian Supremacy and its consequential phenomena: Spiritual Violence, Spiritual Terrorism, Religious Abuse, and ultimately, Spiritual Trauma.

The possibility to transform these realities is directly linked to the ability to recognize and name experiences of religion-based violence in its many forms. Language and conceptual analysis are essential tools towards developing frameworks for dialogical conversation and sustained engagement against violence that is enacted through religion and/or spiritual means. The lack of terminology and theoretical inquiry with which to articulate ourselves at a personal and grassroots level is not arbitrary; it intentionally renders us isolated and our communal experiences indecipherable.

In response, this text aims to conceptualize, define, and unmask the systemic violence of white Christian Supremacy and give respective attention to the wounds and healing processes of those who it preys upon. For that, we must expose the underlying legacy of systemic ideological colonization that propagates shame and fear in order to control, subjugate, and mass produce internalized violence.

Chapter 1 opens the book with an overview of Spiritual Trauma, a phenomenon full of its own complexity and worthy of comprehensive study and research. Though we do not cover all its facets, it is important to name Spiritual Trauma and recognize it as a logical consequence of the violent phenomena developed in the proceeding four chapters.

Chapter 2 delves into the origins of white Christian Supremacy in the Americas since the arrival of European colonizers over 500 years ago and its pervasive and continued influence at every level of communal life.

Chapter 3 describes how white Christian Supremacy results in everyday, normalized practices of Spiritual Violence, how it manifests at different levels of society, and how it gets internalized over time. We will then address the connections between Spiritual Violence, patriarchy, and the weaponization of the biblical text.

Chapter 4 explores an extreme form of Spiritual Violence which is aptly called Spiritual Terrorism, because it is meant to control its victims by keeping them in a state of extreme perpetual fear through the constant threat of violence from many different axes of power at once.

Chapter 5 delves into the many ways in which the leadership roles and cultural environment of religious institutions play a big part in Religious Abuse, alongside examples of how Christian theological ideas are embodied in behaviors that contribute to the epidemic of abuse in our communities of faith.

Methodologically, each chapter aspires to honor the various ways of knowing beyond the facts-based, logic-centered mind. Because these are real violences that impact people's lives, an ethnographic approach helps us better understand the experiences of survivors who have struggled with the religious phenomenon analyzed in each section. Some narratives are fictionalized composites of real testimonies that add living flesh to the conceptual bones of the analytical work. Other times, they are direct, first-hand accounts of one individual's lived experience. All are true. They show rather than tell the living wounds and scars that religion-based violence leaves on the body, mind, and soul.

Because this material can be emotionally heavy or psychologically triggering for some, I encourage readers to take care of themselves and engage with the material as it feels appropriate in your body. There are moments to pause for reflection practices in the Sentipensar body sections to help process the emotions that may come up in the conceptual analysis and personal narratives.

We recognize the centrality of the body as possessing deep knowledge, and we honor its personal and generational memory. Dr. Judith Bautista Fajardo developed body practices for each chapter in the Spanish language edition that utilize relaxation, self-observation, and guided movement exercises to track the traces of trauma in our bodily memory and give them channels for expression and release. Content from the Sentipensar body practice sections is translated renderings of these original texts.

We feel it is irresponsible to focus solely on the problem without attending to the process of healing. Thus, relevant chapters contain useful offerings in the appendices on how to identify our lived experiences with Spiritual Violence and some practical strategies of where to begin our healing journey for those who have experienced them. Taken directly from the content of the Spanish version of this book, these are well-worn pathways that are humbly offered here in the hope that they will be adapted and enriched by others.

Finally, the book closes with a visual analogy of a weapons factory to illustrate the book's concepts in relation to each other. By imagining white Christian Supremacy as a weapons factory, the text traces how sacred sources—such as the Bible, church doctrine, and Christian tradition—are extracted from their liberative contexts and refashioned into weapons of Spiritual Violence.

Through this framework, the book identifies multiple forms of Spiritual Violence, ranging from every day microaggressions to intimate spiritual and physical abuse, communal terror, internalized self-destruction, and large-scale atrocities such as colonization and genocide. Each "weapon" represents a different scale and intention of harm, yet all emerge from the same ideological machinery of white Christian Supremacy. Together, the analogy exposes how power and religion collude to normalize domination, obscure accountability, and inflict lasting damage on bodies, communities, and entire peoples.

Readers are invited to turn to the back of book to encounter the full visual rendering of this analogy with a deeper exploration of how these concepts unfold in detail. I recognize that this content is difficult to read and can be triggering for sensitive readers. Nevertheless, this visual analogy is apropos for the subject matter it represents. The dire consequences of white Christian Supremacy are not theoretical; they are real physical, psychological, and spiritual violences. People are suffering and dying every day. This is one of the most critical concerns of our generation. Recovering the body and spirit from white Christian Supremacy cannot wait until Heaven.

We offer this content with the intention of building solidarity and common ground in our conceptual understanding of religion-based violence across the Americas. Sharing with each other across languages, cultures, and geographies can help us better articulate our shared struggles as well as expand the possibilities for a more united resistance movement. Our goal is to end religion-based violence from inside and outside religious institutions, and we hope to cultivate allies and accomplices in the work—Christians and non-Christians alike—people of conscience across borders, denominations, cultures, and language.

This is your invitation to join us.

1: Spiritual Trauma

Public awareness of trauma has increased significantly over the past several decades, yet trauma is still most often understood as the domain of psychology and the health sciences. While trauma is indeed a psychological phenomenon requiring clinical expertise, it is also a deeply spiritual concern—particularly in cases of religion-based violence. Spiritual Violence penetrates the body even when its wounds are invisible. Such violence emerges from ideologies that harden into beliefs, become encoded in language, and ultimately manifest as practices that assault personhood and erode human dignity.

As a spiritual activist and Christian pastor, I have sat with LGBTQIA+ communities and listened to their stories of Spiritual Violence on six continents for more than two decades. These violences take many forms—physical, psychological, emotional, economic—but as one whose vocation is to care for the life of the spirit, I have come to recognize a critical dimension of harm that remains largely unattended. Too often, we fail to assess the profound repercussions of violence enacted against the spirit in the name of God, or to reckon with the enduring trauma produced by such violence.

One reason for this neglect is the absence of shared language to describe the invisible wounds that strike at the core of our being—our spirit and our sense of self. Many survivors struggle to name what has harmed us or to articulate precisely what continues to ache. Compounding this injury, those who suffer are frequently led to believe that the harm we experience is our own fault.

As a theologian, I enter the interdisciplinary conversation on trauma to examine how political power and religious ideology converge to corrupt the sacred and the spiritual. Although trauma and healing are well-established areas of study, religion-based trauma demands a more nuanced theological framework. Here we offer such a framework by naming Spiritual Violence, tracing its roots in the ideologies of white Christian Supremacy, and examining the violent practices these ideologies authorize and sustain.

Rather than proceeding linearly—from ideology to violent action, to traumatic consequence—we begin with the body. Specifically, I attend to the ways Spiritual Trauma inhabits the body and threatens the lives of those who experience it. By starting here, we foreground the lived realities of survivors and resist abstractions that distance theology from embodied suffering.

Most of us will encounter at least one traumatic event over the course of our lives. In addition, all of us carry the legacies of generational trauma—encoded biologically, socially, and environmentally—within our bodies. While such events are often unavoidable, the ways individuals and communities respond to them play a decisive role in whether difficult experiences become long-term trauma.

There is no formula that guarantees immunity from trauma. Whether harm becomes traumatic is deeply personal and context-specific. Two people may experience the same event and respond in markedly different ways. Even the same person may respond differently to similar experiences at different stages of life. Trauma is shaped by factors such as age, prior exposure to harm, economic precarity, mental health, and access to supportive relationships and resources. It is also influenced by the intensity, duration, and repetition of the harm, as well as by who—or what—caused it.

From a psychological perspective, trauma is commonly defined as follows:

> Trauma is any disturbing experience that results in significant fear, confusion, disassociation, helplessness or other disruptive feelings intense enough to have a long-lasting negative effect on a person's attitudes, behavior, or other aspects of functioning.
>
> Traumatic events include those caused by human behavior (e.g. rape, war, industrial accidents) as well as by nature (e.g. earthquakes) and often challenge an individual's view of the world as a just, safe, and predictable place.[5]

From a theological perspective, spirituality is not peripheral but central to personhood and resilience. It is often a primary resource people draw upon when navigating challenging and painful experiences. For this reason, Spiritual Violence is particularly devastating. When God, sacred texts, or religious authorities are positioned as perpetrators—or used as justifications for harm—survivors are stripped of a vital protective factor against trauma and denied a crucial source of healing. Not only are we alienated from personal spiritual practices such as prayer, but we are also cut off from faith communities that might otherwise provide care, meaning, and solidarity.

Spiritual Trauma, then, refers to the trauma experienced by

those who have been subjected to Spiritual Violence, Religious Abuse, and/or Spiritual Terrorism. It produces varied negative consequences that interfere with one's capacity to live freely and fully. Spiritual Trauma often manifests as persistent fear, distrust, confusion, anger, grief, or a sense of abandonment, frequently accompanied by physical symptoms that can escalate into serious medical and mental health conditions.

For this reason, survivor testimony is indispensable. Engaging with survivors' own words allows us to grasp the embodied and spiritual consequences of Spiritual Violence. The following narrative is Nadia's first-person account of Spiritual Trauma resulting from Religious Abuse. Her story illustrates how the harm of religion-based violence does not end when one exits the abusive context. Rather, departure often marks the beginning of a long journey toward healing, resurrection, and restoration.

NADIA[6]

I grew up in a non-practicing Catholic family and struggled from a young age with depression, anxiety, panic attacks, and eating disorders. Back then, I didn't have the language or support to understand that mental health is multifactorial, shaped by biology, environment, life experiences, and development. Instead, I believed my struggles were a sign of personal failure, so I assumed I was simply broken.

Looking for healing, I began attending a neo-Pentecostal evangelical church with my cousins. There I found belonging, purpose, and structure. The church became my safe place. I fell in love with God and the Bible, took every course offered, read every book I could find, and began dreaming of dedicating my life to ministry. Faith gave me community and stability. It made the world feel safe.

When I was eighteen, I was invited to interpret for a famous international pastor visiting Mexico for a miracle crusade. The church service was massive; unlike anything I had ever seen. People screamed, cried, convulsed, and collapsed. I was told this was the power of the Holy Spirit working through the prophet. That same day, he asked if I was of legal age and invited me to travel across the world to serve in his church. I was filled with adrenaline and wonder after everything I had witnessed, but my mother was suspicious and uneasy. It seemed too good to be true. It would be my first time leaving my country, let alone the continent. It took a lot of convincing, but eventually my mom and I agreed. This was a once-in-a-lifetime opportunity. It was my dream to give my life to God.

When I arrived, the world I entered was both awe-inspiring and unsettling. On one hand, I witnessed miracles everywhere. People praised the prophet for healing the impossible: the blind could see, the deaf could hear, people stood up from their wheelchairs and walked away. But on the other hand, I began to see his violent side. He hit people when they annoyed him. He humiliated his disciples in public. He decided when we slept; we would regularly go days on end without a full night's rest. He controlled what and when we ate.

One day, he told me to hand over my antidepressants. Soon after, he took my glasses, saying it was "a step of faith." He told me I had to let these things go if I wanted God to heal and deliver me.

These demands left me vulnerable—physically and emotionally. I started to wonder, *Have I had mental health struggles because I have been possessed my entire life? Is my poor eyesight a sign that my faith is not strong enough?* I felt increasingly insecure. My body was reacting too. I was dizzy, tired, and disconnected from myself. I couldn't reconcile the contradictions I was experiencing: *If the prophet is God's representative on Earth, does that mean God is like him? Does God have that kind of temper?*

Despite everything, I clung to my faith. I believed God loved me. I believed everything would be okay and that it all had a purpose.

One day, the prophet called me into his office. He asked me to sit down and told me that God had revealed something to him about me. He was serious, with disappointment on his face. Then he repeated things I had only told God in prayer. The things he brought up felt deeply shameful to me—my "sexual sin" and the doubts I carried regarding my sexuality. He used words I had only ever spoken in silent moments of prayer. I felt betrayed by God. *Why would God share that with him? Is that the only thing God has to say about me?*

I felt nauseous and dizzy, my heart racing. I felt like an embarrassment to God—exposed and more alone than ever. It felt like a scene from a movie where bullies read a girl's diary aloud, except here, the bully was the prophet, and God was the one who handed over the diary. I wondered, *If there are only two sides, and God, the Creator of the Universe, is on his side, what hope is there for me?*

Something in me broke that day. I couldn't find a reason to live if God didn't love me. I didn't want to eat. I barely moved.

Some days later, the prophet called me to his office again. It was a Sunday, and everyone else in the church was busy preparing for the weekly service. He made sure no one was around and locked the door. He hugged me tightly. At first, I thought he was trying to comfort me, but very quickly I realized he was holding me down with force. Then he sexually assaulted me.

If he had done anything like that even just two weeks earlier, I would have resisted and fought back. I would have screamed and ran away. But at that point, I had no strength left. My psychological, spiritual, and physical defenses were gone—and he knew that. My faith, which had been the most important and sacred part of my identity, was fatally wounded.

Not long after that, through a series of miracles and struggles, my family managed to bring me home. Returning was one of the hardest things I had ever done. Even though every part of my body screamed that he was not a safe person and that I was lucky to have escaped, a part of me still felt like I was letting God down. Like I had failed my mission. Like I should have fought harder, stayed longer, endured more.

I was finally home, but the journey had only begun. The Religious Abuse and Spiritual Violence I experienced had reshaped my life in ways I could not yet understand. My spirit felt injured, and although I was surrounded by people who loved me, none of them had the tools to grasp the impact of what I had survived.

My sense of purpose was gone. I had constant nightmares and intrusive thoughts about being possessed, abandoned by God, and in Hell. I doubted my own judgment. My memories felt blurred, and my body no longer felt like my own. Panic attacks became constant, and depression took over. I struggled to eat, sleep, or talk with others. I spent most of my time alone and on high alert.

It took a long time before I could speak about what had happened during my time in the cult. When I finally did, hearing another Christian say, "I believe you, and what happened to you was wrong. That was not God's will for you," gave me the courage to seek help. As I began researching my symptoms, I found a name that finally explained my experience: Complex Post-Traumatic Stress Disorder (C-PTSD).

Here is what I learned:

> From current research, C-PTSD is understood as the result of prolonged and repeated exposure to trauma, often in relationships where escape or protection is limited, rather than a single traumatic event as in typical PTSD. People with C-PTSD develop complex survival patterns that reshape how they see themselves, others, and the world. Unlike PTSD, which often involves re-experiencing one specific event or sudden fear responses, C-PTSD alters the deeper architecture of a person's inner world. It can distort identity, make emotions feel overwhelming or unreachable, and disrupt trust, safety, and connection. Symptoms often include deep shame, emotional dysregulation, chronic hypervigilance, and difficulties with intimacy.
>
> Trauma research also shows that people who experience repeated harm tied to spiritual or religious beliefs –such as survivors of sexual abuse in religious settings or those subjected to "conversion therapy"– are more likely to develop C-PTSD rather than typical PTSD.
>
> Spiritual Trauma often unfolds over long

> periods of time and develops within religious institutions that hold deep authority over a person's identity, morality, and sense of belonging. These environments create conditions of chronic fear, coercion, shame, and authoritarian control, the same prolonged and entrapping dynamics known to produce C-PTSD.[7]

In the decade that followed, I spoke with pastors, therapists, feminist advocates, and other survivors in an effort to make sense of it all. Each carried pieces of wisdom I needed for my healing, and I wove them together to tend to my body, mind, and spirit.

Even now, there are things I still do not fully understand. I have tried to dismiss the memories of the supernatural things I witnessed, searching for logical explanations so I could write it all off as fake—the healings, the spirit work, the miracles. But the truth is, I can't, nor do I want to. That would not be true to myself: I still believe in miracles.

Even with all my unanswered questions, there is one thing I know for sure: God is not like him. God does not think of me the way he did. God sustained me during that time. God embraces my whole self—including my sexuality, which is a gift, not a flaw. God is always on the side of the hurting. For me, holding onto that truth is a radical act of faith. No one can take that from me again. I remind myself often: *I am loved unconditionally by the One who created me in Their image.*

Spiritual Trauma from Religious Abuse

Although Spiritual Trauma does not exclusively result from Religious Abuse, the severity and prolonged nature of Religious Abuse frequently lead to Spiritual Trauma. Trauma is not synonymous with the triggering event itself; rather, it is the residue of violence imprinted on the body, psyche, and spirit. Trauma is unprocessed somatic memory—experience that remains unfinished because it has not yet been fully named, understood, or healed.

If Spiritual Trauma can be understood as a lingering state of paralysis in body, mind, and spirit following Spiritual Violence, then one reason it becomes lodged so deeply is that survivors are often unable to recognize or comprehend the abuse they have endured. When violence is cloaked in religious language and justified by harmful theologies, it becomes exceedingly difficult to identify it as violence at all. Naming Spiritual Violence and acknowledging its consequences are therefore essential steps on the path toward healing.

In the next section we will delve into the religious beliefs that hinder survivors from recognizing harm in the first place and then punish them for disclosing it once they do come forward. Both inside and outside of the religious community, victim-blaming is common. Survivors are harshly judged for "allowing" abuse to happen or for not leaving the situation sooner. Nadia will continue her reflection from above responding to this reality, not only from her own experiences as a survivor of Religious Abuse, but also as a theologian, an LGBTQIA+ activist, and someone who educates and accompanies other survivors of Spiritual Trauma.

"Why Didn't You Just Leave?"[8]

There are many ways to answer this question, and each perspective reveals a different part of the survivor experience. Research in evolutionary psychology, social neuroscience, and anthropology shows that the need to belong is a basic human motivation. Threats to belonging activate brain regions associated with physical pain and survival alarms, and emotions like fear of rejection, guilt, shame, and strong peer pressure function as internal warning systems to prevent social exclusion. Because of this, many of us tolerate discomfort or are even willing to risk something bad happening [repeatedly] if it helps preserve group membership: our biology is deeply oriented toward maintaining connection.

These biological and psychological dynamics interact with the social reality that churches often serve as community centers, childcare providers, friend groups, extended family, and emotional support systems. Leaving can mean losing not only one's spiritual community but also one's entire social world: relationships, practical resources, safety nets, and identity. That loss can feel overwhelming and even as destabilizing as the abuse itself.

Theological teachings can make this even harder such as linking suffering, obedience, and sacrifice with holiness, encouraging people to see harm as something they must endure to grow in faith. Survivors are often taught that unquestioning obedience is a virtue, that leaders know better, and that their own instincts are untrustworthy.

In many Christian contexts, people are taught to ignore the warning signs in their bodies or to distrust their own protective instincts. Messages like "the heart is deceitful" or "do not follow the flesh" can train us to silence our intuition, especially when it contradicts what authority figures demand. We are conditioned to doubt everything before we ever consider doubting God, or those who claim to speak on God's behalf.

This has profound consequences for how people understand harm, and what we believe is possible in response to it. When abuse is spiritualized, and when the institutions or figures responsible for it are treated as sacred or beyond reproach, it becomes nearly impossible to imagine justice. The idea that change could happen—that accountability is even an option—can feel naive or futile. For many, the result is a deep and painful hopelessness: the sense that harm must simply be endured in silence, rather than named or challenged. Even if we have a spiritual community, we either fade into oblivion or risk our own reputation. Regardless, grief often ensues.

Every survivor's story is different, and the circumstances that shape our ability to stay or leave vary widely. This is precisely why the question "Why didn't you just leave?" is so often revictimizing. It rarely reflects genuine curiosity or care; instead, it shifts blame onto the survivor while oversimplifying complex dynamics that take years to recognize, unlearn, and heal from.

A Culture of Faithful Silence

From the outside, it may seem reasonable to ask why someone would remain in a community that causes them harm or why they would suffer in silence rather than report abuse. In reality, the reasons are complex and deeply practical. For many, the church is not only the center of spiritual life but also the primary site of social belonging, family connection, and community reputation.

While public disclosure can sometimes empower others to recognize and name their own experiences, reporting rates remain exceedingly low. Survivors often calculate—accurately—that speaking out may be more detrimental to themselves and to the community than remaining silent.

Particularly in cases where the violence or abuse is sexual in nature, victims are frequently groomed in ways that exploit trust, devotion, and vulnerability. These dynamics are then contorted to frame abuse as the victim's fault—evidence of moral failure or sexual sin. Women and girls in particular, are subjected to deeply gendered spiritual shaming, labeled as temptresses, seductresses, or bearers of a "Jezebel spirit." When survivors do come forward, we are often blamed for seducing the "men of God" and required to confess and repent, while perpetrators escape accountability.

Compounding this harm is the internalization of theological mandates to submit to authority. Many victims learn to distrust our own perceptions rather than question systems designed to concentrate power in religious leaders. The widespread assumption that clergy and churches are inherently righteous further undermines confidence in our own lived experiences. This is especially true when a leader is charismatic with spiritual gifts and effective as a teacher or preacher. Our own spiritual encounters under their leadership convince us that they are good and divinely appointed, making it difficult to believe they could cause harm, even if it happened to us directly.

Other times victims don't disclose abuse because they believe the pastor is untouchable. Even when survivors speak clearly and truthfully, their credibility is often weighed against that of the accused faith leader. Children are dismissed as confused or manipulated; adults are accused of bitterness or rebellion. Institutional responses, when they occur at all, are typically handled quietly, behind closed doors, and without transparency, accountability, or restitution.

Spiritual beliefs themselves also function as barriers to disclosure. Many communities teach that salvation depends on remaining under proper spiritual authority or that we need an intermediary between us and God. Many of us fear that our salvation is at stake when leaving a church or accusing a faith leader—one of "God's chosen"—of harm. We are led to believe that we need spiritual covering and guidance, so leaving a church or challenging a leader may be framed as rebellion against God. In such contexts, confronting abuse can feel too dangerous to surmount.

Challenging religious leaders can feel like challenging God directly, which for most believers has apocalyptic consequences. The very image of God that we have been given in church can easily lend itself to power and abuse. Understanding God as the supreme Creator, loving Father, and cosmic Judge, alongside counter images of the Divine as the punisher and annihilator of entire civilizations gets transposed onto our understanding about how relationship dynamics should be between humans.

For example, as Christians, we cling to the belief that God loves us above all else, and in response, we are supposed to love God in return; yet it is considered normal and appropriate for us to fear God's jealousy, anger, and wrath. We are taught that God regularly punishes us and tests our faith; yet, we are supposed to welcome it with gratitude and submission. It becomes our responsibility to not provoke God's ire, rather than God's responsibility to regulate their own emotions and violence. When we do something wrong according to this ideology, God shows us mercy, kindness, and forgiveness only in response to our submission and repentance.

These dominant images of God often mirror and legitimize abusive power dynamics. The normalization of fear, punishment, and submission in divine-human relationships makes it difficult to recognize similar dynamics as abusive when enacted by religious leaders.

These patterns are reinforced when churches reject "secular" frameworks for understanding consent, power, mental health, and abuse. Appeals to Scripture—particularly Paul's injunctions to the church at Corinth against involving outside authorities—are used to discourage reporting and continues to be widely observed by Christian communities of faith. This rejection of the outside world, alongside the belief that the secular world is ruled by evil and persecutes Christians, prohibits both victims and church communities from seeking help from authorities and outside sources. In these cases, fear becomes an effective tool to keep violence hidden, abuse silenced, and victims complying.

Mental health struggles are likewise moralized, interpreted as spiritual failure, demonic influence, or insufficient faith. Many faith communities believe that if we have Jesus, true believers should be happy all the time. Depression, anxiety, PTSD, trauma responses, and the like are considered symptoms of a godless life. These theological ideas, alongside those that glorify suffering as salvific and lift up adversity as a test of faith to be endured, further entrench silence and self-blame.

Finally, forgiveness is a theological precept that has been enshrined among believers as the only Christian, spiritually acceptable response to harm. Teachings on turning the other cheek, loving one's enemies, or seventy-times-seven forgiveness are often weaponized to demand compliance from those who have experienced violence. In these communities, God alone is responsible for passing judgement, demanding restitution, and providing accountability—all of which are entirely independent of the victim. Here, it is God who has been wronged and whose honor has been offended, and it is only God who can set it right.

Within this framework, anger, rage, resentment, and grief are not honored for what they are: normal, expected responses to violence. Instead, they are pathologized as spiritual immaturity. Forgiveness, in this context, becomes not a path to healing, but a means of control that prioritizes institutional stability over survivor well-being.

Together, these dynamics reveal why Spiritual Trauma is so difficult to address. Moral formation rooted in obedience undermines trust in embodied knowledge. We become so highly attuned to the expectations and will of others that we can lose ourselves in the process.

Next, hierarchical authority constrains agency. The power dynamics of religious spaces conflate our commitment to God with our submission to authoritative figures within the legalistic religious frameworks used to maintain control. Here, telling the truth about our experiences of Spiritual Violence can feel like disloyalty to God.

Lastly, speaking up, seeking help, or even naming the harm can feel like a betrayal of everything we have been taught. It often means stepping into a position of defiance toward the very community that, in many cases, is our primary or only network of support. After all the time, energy, creativity and money that individuals invest in our communities of faith, it is understandable that these conditions would lead many to hold out hope that the situation will get better. In conjunction with valid fears of not being believed, being humiliated, having our reputation ruined or being physically harmed, silence appears safer than resistance.

SENTIPENSAR: SPIRITUAL LIFE MAP

Identifying how common Christian theologies have impacted our lives and contributed to violence we have suffered is an emotionally charged topic, because it touches some of our most vulnerable life experiences. It's normal for some of us to have feelings of hostility or resentment towards Christianity, or to distance ourselves from religion entirely.

Others of us have chosen to seek change within religious institutions. There is no one "right" way; the paths of healing are many and diverse. We can shift and turn and re/turn as many times as needed as we figure out what feels best for our own lives. Whatever route our spiritual journey takes, we carry the emotional consequences of these winding paths inside ourselves.

It might be helpful to take a moment to map your own spiritual journey and then share some of your story. Don't forget to include pivotal moments of discovery, decisions you have made along the way, and the feelings you associate with them.

In the Absence of the Body

Trauma disrupts presence. Survivors may become trapped in cycles of fear, shame, rage, or dissociation. Trauma alters memory, perception, and nervous system functioning. Its effects manifest physically in myriad ways, from addictive numbing behaviors (eating disorders, high-risk activities, substance abuse, etc.) to mental illness (depression, anxiety, etc.) to chronic and life-threatening disease (autoimmune diseases, cardiovascular conditions, chronic pain, cancer, etc.). Symptoms may recede and reemerge as the body responds to new triggers.[9]

While dissociation may serve as a short-term survival strategy, it is not sustainable. Though many of us were indoctrinated to disregard it entirely, the body holds wisdom and memory, and healing requires attentiveness to both. Liberation, therefore, must be embodied.

Integrated healing demands attention to mind, body, and spirit. Mental health professionals, alongside communities of care, are essential companions on this journey. Theologies of liberation can help dismantle the self-erasing logics of white Christian Supremacy and cultivate life-affirming, body-honoring spiritualities. To say it outright:

Silence produces disconnection.

Disconnection fosters bodily absence.

Yet the body cannot be liberated

until we understand how it was lost.

The work of returning to the body is inseparable from the work of tending to the spiritual harm and trauma endured. Healing, however, requires more than attention or care—it requires us to diagnose and name. Spiritual Trauma cannot be addressed apart from the ideological conditions that produced it. The following chapter traces the origins, development, and deployment of white Christian Supremacy as a theological construct that captures the imagination, disciplines the body, and generates profound spiritual harm.

2: White Christian Supremacy

To comprehend the magnitude of Spiritual Violence and the Spiritual Trauma that comes from it, we must first situate it within a larger framework of supremacy that makes its death-dealing impact so powerful. In the Western Hemisphere, the political and social conditions that make spiritual violences possible today began with the arrival of the European colonizers and their Christian imperialism over five centuries ago.

Religious hegemony describes the phenomenon in which the religious values, systems of belief, and/or cultural ethos from a dominant religion creates the foundation for what is commonly considered "normal" and "good." In our context, Christianity—encompassing Catholicism, Protestantism, and Evangelicalism—presides as the hegemonic force that shapes all aspects of a society. This includes the educational, political, legal, social, and economic structures of a country or region, even if it is structured as secular or claims to be areligious. Thus Christian hegemony affects everyone, regardless of one's own faith or culture.

The predominance of cultural Christianity in our region is not the result of an indigenous spirituality or the organic spread of a faith tradition, but rather, the consequence of *conquista,* colonization, and settler colonialism brought by European powers through their violent process of Christian conquest and conversion. This religious imposition affected all levels of society such that, in the present day, it continues to mark the standards of morality and rhythms of social life, establishing holy days like Christmas and Easter and cultural rites of passage like baptism, first communion, and marriage, among others.

white Christian Supremacy is possible because of the prevalence of Christian hegemony, but they are not synonymous. white Christian Supremacy reproduces violence in many forms—both spiritual and physical in nature—by stealing the sacred texts, religious imagery, and traditions of Christianity and then deploying them as weaponized religion. Historically, we can identify a kind of parasitic relationship between systems of domination, such as white supremacy, and the strains of Christianity that they feed off. white Christian Supremacy co-ops religious language and culture and twists it to justify the violent and oppressive actions of governments, institutions, powerful interest groups and privileged individuals.

The ideologies of white Christian Supremacy work in patterns of false binaries that generally discourage nuance, open dialogue across difference, and the exploration of diversity as a creative and positive reflection of the natural world. This framework typically uses fear, shame, and coercion to gain followers. By aggressively sorting and segregating everything and everyone into predetermined boxes of good or evil, greater than or lesser than, it impedes Christians from questioning or developing our own ways of experiencing God or the world beyond white Christian Supremacy's own logic systems. It manipulates

Christian language and culture to maintain control and keep its systems of power firmly in place at every level of society. Ideologies of white Christian Supremacy are frequently applied to moralize harmful political maneuvers, validate the actions of violent institutions and systems, encourage exclusion, and legitimate the unequal distribution of natural resources and access to safety and basic necessities.

white Christian Supremacy is not "Christianity;" it is a perverted abuse of the religion that maliciously exploits human and natural resources to create a system of domination that targets anyone and anything that could challenge its superiority.

Origins of white Christian Supremacy in the Americas

As the followers of the teachings of Jesus of Nazareth (originally called 'Nazarenes' or the pejorative, 'Christians') coalesced from a motley crew of scattered communities with diverse faith practices and teachings into a standardized, government-sanctioned, mainstream religion at the Council of Nicaea in 325 CE, they laid the political underpinnings for white Christian Supremacy. In 380 CE, Christianity, as defined by the Council of Nicaea, became the official religion of the Roman Empire. It was immediately used by those in power to deem all other sects of Christianity heretical and therefore illegal. Their land and assets were promptly confiscated by the Roman Empire, and their followers persecuted in the name of the Christian god.[10]

Since then, elements of Christianity have been manipulated by those with political, economic, and religious power to quell opposition and moralize their own self-serving ends. From the persecution of Christian heretics, to the Crusades, to the war on witches and the Inquisition, to the countless political disputes for land and power, there have been innumerable millions of victims of violence, subjugation, and ultimately death—all legitimized by a kind of Christianity forced to serve the egomaniacal will of powerful men.

Across the Americas, white Christian Supremacy arrived with the colonial powers of Western Europe during the "Age of Discovery" in the fifteenth century. Their project of conquest and colonization was not only an economic and political operation to confiscate the natural and human resources of the region, it also came wrapped in the blessing and mandate of the Church. Under the guise of Christian missions, they invaded lands already inhabited by diverse peoples possessing their own rich social, cultural, economic, and religious ecosystems.

Unlike most of the pre-Columbian civilizations of the Americas where the worship of a new reigning deity was incorporated into a polytheistic cosmology of local religious myths and rituals, conversion to Christianity demanded the total annihilation of indigenous spiritualities.

Every military intervention was preceded by the demand to adopt the new religion—Christianity—under threat of death, imposed in the name of the Christian god with the approval of the Church. The original inhabitants of the land experienced genocide, rape, enslavement, and the systematic dismantling of their beliefs, cultures, and ways of life… an apocalypse. As they were brought under the conditions of slavery, they forever lost the possibility of sovereignty over their own lands, lives, bodies, and children.

One of the first casualties of white Christian Supremacy in

Abya Yala was human dignity as the people native to these lands were exploited and discarded in mass. Colonial interests are responsible for the murder of tens of millions of Indigenous people—genocides of up to 95% of the native population in some areas of the Americas—due to invasion, enslavement, and disease. When Brown Indigenous bodies and souls were not sufficient for the insatiable demands of colonial gluttony, Black Indigenous bodies and souls were stolen and trafficked from the African continent. More than 12 million people were kidnapped from their home nations in Africa and forced into chattel slavery in the Caribbean Islands and across the Americas.

All of this facilitated the consolidation of European wealth and power by force backed by Christianity. In this worldview, Europeans were more civilized, and therefore, morally superior. The complete supremacy of their religion and way of life provided the moral justification for the brutal subjugation of the Americas under the semblance of missionization. They believed they were especially chosen by God to subdue and dominate the entire world for the purpose of its salvation, even if it came with the promise of death for entire civilizations.[11]

Doctrines of Christian Discovery

Some of the most important political documents in this endeavor were a series of religious decrees called papal bulls issued by the Vatican in the 15th century. These are some of the best examples of how white Christian Supremacy operates; Christianity twisted and perverted to serve the political and economic powers of the time.

The papal bull, *Dum Diversas*, was issued by Pope Nicholas V in 1452 and authorized the king of Portugal

> "to invade, search out, capture, vanquish, and subdue all Saracens [Muslims] and pagans whatsoever, and other enemies of Christ wheresoever placed, and the kingdoms...possessions, and all movable and immovable goods whatsoever held and possessed by them and to reduce their persons to perpetual slavery..."[12]

thus launching the buying and selling of human beings through the West African slave trade with the Church's blessing.

Romanus Pontifex, another papal bull issued by the same pope in 1455, gave Catholic nations of Europe the right to seize all land and goods in the "New World" not already belonging to another Christian European monarch, and it encouraged the enslavement of native, non-Christian peoples in Africa and the Americas.

Lastly, the *Inter Caetera*, issued by Pope Alexander VI in 1493, settled land disputes between the Spanish and Portuguese monarchs over ownership of the Americas and celebrated them for

> "elevating the Catholic faith and the Christian religion, especially in [these] our times, as well as extending and spreading it everywhere, securing the salvation of souls and subduing the barbarous nations and bringing them back to the faith itself."[13]

These official decrees from the Pope, the highest authority of the Catholic Church, declared non-Christians "enemies of Christ"—first in Africa and then the Americas—and commissioned the Christian monarchs of Europe to steal the lands and possessions, exploit the natural and human resources, brutally conquer and enslave all non-Christian peoples, and take full dominion over any territory not already owned by another Christian [European] kingdom.

Together, these declarations created the political and legal basis as well as the moral justification for the Doctrines of Christian Discovery, a framework that is still being used against Indigenous peoples today. The Doctrines of Christian Discovery continues to govern international property law in the United States and across the Americas. Furthermore, multinational corporations and governments apply its principles to continue to withhold sovereignty and steal the land and natural resources of Indigenous peoples.[14]

The process of colonization forever marked the formation of a socio-cultural identity based in the religious sensibilities of the white Christian European invaders. The culture of white Christian Supremacy imposed by colonizing people over 500 years ago created an inseparable correlation between political, social, and economic practices of domination and Christian religious beliefs that continue to affect all areas of life today.

From the macro level of society all the way down to the personal and individual, our assumptions of what it means to be a good person are shaped by this legacy. Modern day expectations about what is morally right and wrong, what personal identities are godly and how they should be expressed, and even how we should use our time, talent, and resources are based on categories and religious logics imposed over 500 years ago. The violence this causes to a person or community—both seen and unseen—is at the heart of understanding Spiritual Violence.

SENTIPENSAR: ANALYZING THE SACRED TEXT

Recognizing that almost any aspect of a religion can be distorted and misappropriated to serve those who wield it as a tool for power is the first step in identifying white Christian Supremacy. Remember, the greatest danger lies not in the Bible itself or in Christian doctrines and traditions alone. The harm comes when these are activated to control others and systematically grant privileges to some and deny the rights of others.

A "hermenutic of suspicion" is a term that describes an approach to reading Scripture and analyzing the application of religious language, symbols, and culture that encourages asking questions and delving beneath surface meanings to uncover less obvious contexts and deeper motivations. This is imperative so that we don't fall victim to the schemes of white Christian Supremacy, which would have us believe that questions and concerns are failures of faith rather than necessary tools of faithful discernment.[15]

If you suspect that God or sacred text is being used coercively, here are some key questions to ask yourself:

- Who benefits from this way of thinking or believing?
- Which voices and experiences are not represented here?
- Who has power in this situation and who does not?

NUSCAA

Nuscaa lives and breathes religious syncretism every day of her life. She belongs to one of the many communities of Mayan peoples and walks the lands her ancestors walked. Their blood runs strong in her veins, in the shape of her nose, and in the color of her flesh. Since before she can remember, she has learned the rituals and wisdom teachings of the ancestors from her grandmother, her mother, and the other women in their community.

Nevertheless, Nuscaa's Mayan community exists within a Christian world. At school, she received the required curriculum in religion and history. She took her first communion alongside her peers. She has enjoyed the religious festivals throughout the year in the plaza in front of the parish church and has always participated in the Holy Week processions and Christmas pageants.

She has been a part of both worlds, and both worlds have felt like they were part of her. Internally, they lived together in harmony; Jesus of Nazareth is part of the cosmology of wise ancestors. As a child, she loved to hear the stories about their acts of heroism and how they always cared for the most vulnerable... "the least of these." The passing of time was recorded in her life by the memories of sacred rituals and family gatherings according to the holy days of the Catholic church, while the language and practices themselves were deeply Mayan.

For example, their planting and harvest rituals occur on important feast days of Catholic saints and their ceremonies always begin with incense and the Lord's Prayer and Ave Marias. Their altars are filled with offerings of flowers, food, bread, chocolate, amaranth, and distilled spirits, laid alongside rosaries and images of Jesus on the cross, Catholic saints, Our Lady of Guadalupe, and framed photos of family members who have passed into the land of the ancestors.

Although their Indigenous practices would never be authorized officially by the Church, all the priests knew about them and sometimes even attended their *danzas* and *fiestas*. Some of the priests over the years have even been Maya, and to her, all Mayas are Catholic. This blended spirituality was generally accepted by the wider community, though Nuscaa sometimes experienced discrimination when people looked down on her family for wearing traditional clothes, speaking their Indigenous language, and having darker skin. She felt determined to show everyone that she was just as smart and could speak Spanish just as well as anyone else, and that she could also honor her community in the traditional ways.

When Nuscaa was 14 years old, foreign missionaries came into their community. They weren't familiar with the ways of the Mayas, and they condemned all Indigenous practices as superstition and witchcraft. They blamed many social ills on this kind of "blasphemy." The missionaries only came for a short while, but the hostility of local Christians grew and intensified as economic conditions worsened. Soon after, the elders of the community decided that their rituals would be closed to outsiders and done only in their private homes.

Before the next ceremony, Nuscaa could feel the tension in the early morning air as palpable as the coming rain. As she helped the spiritual guides prepare the altar and the corn offerings, every prayer was a plea of intersession, "Please. Come to us. Be with us. Help us." Nuscaa prayed to Jesus and to the ancestors. She could feel the fear surrounding her people. The communal tasks helped to ground her and seemed to settle everyone else as well. They mostly worked in silence, finding intimacy and peace in sharing the familiar rhythmic tasks of cleaning and decorating their sacred space.

Over the next few days, their rituals went as they always had, though smaller and more solemn than she remembered from past years.

The next morning, the town was abuzz with people gossiping in hushed voices. Nuscaa felt the eyes of many on her and her sisters as they entered the park in the square, but before they could even begin their errands, one of their cousins caught sight of them and broke into a run. Through sobs she explained that their great-uncle, Izamal, had died. She didn't know what had happened exactly, but there were rumors that the neighbors were upset because of the ceremonies and had set his house on fire to purge the evil spirits and *demonios*. No matter how it started, no one had gone to help; the body of Tío Izamal was embraced by the fire, along with his humble belongings.

Even as the family made funeral preparations, they already knew that no one would ever be held responsible for the fire or their uncle's death. Nuscaa wondered if they would still perform the Mayan parts of the ceremonies to lay her great-uncle to rest. She wasn't even sure she could pick out which parts were the Mayan ones and which ones were the Catholic ones. She still couldn't wrap her mind around it. *How is it possible to be a Christian and harbor so much anger and hatred in your heart? Who could possibly believe that allowing someone to die would make God happy? Who could believe that Jesus would bless this when he promised life for his people?*

The women of community, more seasoned in the pain

of grief and loss, surrounded Nuscaa and her cousins with stories that filled her spirit with their eternal truths: beyond human fear and violence, the Great Spirit, the Mother Goddess, the Source of Creation, continues to pour out her blessings, offering strength to mend and create; continuing to labor for the unity and wellbeing of all of Creation. Nuscaa felt the Holy Spirit inside her, and she knew that she was called to uphold the ancient wisdom of her people no matter what was to come.

In the courtyard of her family home, she continues to gather the little ones, telling the same stories that she received from her mother, her grandmother, and Tío Izamal.

SENTIPENSAR: SELF-MASSAGE BODY PRACTICE

With more than 20 generations since Columbus landed on the Caribbean Islands in 1492, we each carry the DNA of over one million direct ancestors since conquest. Whether our ancestors held identities of privilege as "colonizer" or ones of oppression as "colonized/enslaved" or a combination of both, we have all inherited immense generational trauma from our ancestors' experiences of colonization. The devastation of their experiences of violent invasion, land theft, rape, physical-cultural-spiritual genocide, the forced migration and enslavement of African peoples, the subjugation, enslavement, and displacement of Indigenous peoples across the Americas, and the extraction and exportation of natural and human resources by Christian European colonizers are coded into our genes and impact our health and wellbeing even until today.

Once we recognize the traces of trauma in our psyches and in our bodies as a consequence of white Christian Supremacy, we can more easily identify the feelings and manifestations that these wounds provoke in us. From there, it is paramount to offer ourselves spaces for restitution: small, daily actions that nurture our self-love, self-care, and our ability to heal in community.

Among these routines, self-massage is one simple, restorative practice.

For this exercise, we recommend using a small lime or lemon that is not completely ripe and soft. Turn on some background music and create a cozy atmosphere, either in a group or individually. Start by lying down flat on the floor, on a blanket, a mat, or on the grass and then try to release the weight of your body. Become aware of your whole body from the soles of your feet to the crown of your head. Flow into the natural rhythm of your breath entering and exiting your body as you feel the earth beneath you.

Take the lime in one hand and begin your self-massage by using it to make circular movements starting at your head. You can either sit up or remain laying down as you explore your body and the best ways to massage it with the lime. Move down from your head slowly, massaging your whole body. Feel the texture and density of the fruit and enjoy the citrus smell that it leaves on your skin or clothes. If you are in a group, you can ask someone else to use your lime to massage the places you cannot easily reach, such as your back, and you can reciprocate for others.

Once you reach your feet, roll the lime on the floor with the soles of your bare feet. Focus on stimulating the entire sole of your foot, especially the places that may be sensitive or carry tension.

Finally, with a feeling of gratitude, bury or compost the fruit. (Please note that the lime absorbs bacteria and toxins from our bodies, so it should not be consumed.)

The traumas of our ancestors, layered with generations of systemic oppression alongside our own lived experiences can be a heavy spiritual burden. However, we also carry their legacies of resistance, resilience, survival, creativity, joy and love with us wherever we go. And what's more, when we attend to these spiritual wounds and generational traumas in our own lives, we simultaneously heal and transform our lineages as well.

Faith Resisting Empire

Perhaps the most significant miracle of faith is that despite the history of violent colonizing Christianity and the enduring reality of colonial religion today, there have always been people and communities who have resisted and engaged their Christian faith in the work of liberation. In fact, many of us feel called to do the work of justice and healing in the world precisely because of our Christian faith!

While weaponized religion must be contested, it is irresponsible to deny the role of churches and faith institutions in providing life-saving services and refuge to many who would otherwise go without. It is possible to hold the complexity of the "both/and" within our analysis of Christianity; it can both be the motivation to push for life-affirming change and it can also be the basis for wide-scale death. Even as we denounce the harm caused by white Christian Supremacy, we can also recognize the life-giving efforts of many Christians and faith communities.

Countless unnamed Christians have taken the biblical mandate to "love thy neighbor as thyself" to heart and have been part of movements to break the status quo of white Christian Supremacy. Below are just a few examples of past and present acts of faithful resistance:

- Indigenous people who wove their rituals, beliefs, and practices into Christianity through religious syncretism in order to keep them from being erased;

- Women who joined convents to dedicate their lives to intellectual and spiritual scholarship when they did not want to submit to the expected obligatory roles solely as wives and mothers;

- Enslaved Black people who refused to read the Letters of Paul in the Bible because they were used to justify chattel slavery;

- Roman Catholic priests who secretly ordain women into the priesthood;

- Church congregations who provide physical sanctuary to undocumented immigrants;

- Midwives and healers who secretly kept ancient plant medicine and healing ways alive since before biblical times;

- Conscientious objectors who refused to go to war in foreign lands on behalf of imperialist nations;

- Ordained clergy who risk being defrocked for blessing the marriages of Queer couples;

- Christians who engaged in acts of civil disobedience for human dignity and civil rights;

- Faith organizations who advocate for social justice issues like Trans rights, environmental protections, reproductive justice, and abolition of the carceral system.

Additionally, many faith-based social service and charity programs work to address some of the disparities originally caused by ideologies of white Christian Supremacy—even if they do not explicitly acknowledge it as such. It is still the case in many places that churches provide the only social safety net to meet the basic human needs of the most vulnerable in our communities.

In academic traditions, there are a plethora of approaches to theology that contest the colonial legacies of white Christian Supremacy such as Latin American and Black Liberation theologies, Womanist and Mujerista theologies, Queer and Trans theologies, and Feminist and Latin American Feminist theologies, which will be discussed further in chapter five.

Decolonizing Knowledge

The ideologies of white Christian Supremacy are so enmeshed in daily life that they become the default position for what is considered morally right and wrong. Recognizing religion-based violence within the hegemonic religion is very difficult, because the violence has been normalized to the point that it is assumed to be appropriate and good. The more embedded we are in Christianity, the harder it is to detect its harm.

Most people defer to the status quo as objective truths without much examination. However, more often these "truths" are actually the changeable, subjective perceptions of those who have the power to impose their own worldview.

A straightforward example of this is the way that Jesus Christ is mainly depicted in religious art as a peach-skinned white man with blue eyes and golden-brown hair even though this phenotype would be culturally out of place for a Jewish man of the ancient near east over 2,000 years ago. However, in the logic of white Christian Supremacy, the appropriate form for God to embody as a human being is one that mirrors those with historical power and military might in more recent centuries. Thus, the images of Jesus continue to show him with the features of a white European-descended cis-gender man.

One of the most nefarious strategies deployed by systems of domination is to make its logics and histories so ingrained that they become invisible as the default, truth and fact. Thus, the first step in decolonizing our bodies, minds, and spirits from white Christian Supremacy is becoming aware of its existence. Re/membering our personal and collective histories is, in and of itself, rebellion and resistance.

We can re/learn our histories, not as a series of past events that have nothing to do with us today, but rather, as a re/reading of who we are based in how we have been constructed as a society. This requires us to step outside the notion that things are the way they are because "God made them that way" or because that is how God intended them to be. Knowing the ways in which religion has colluded with systems of power to justify mass exploitation, cultural annihilation, and genocide on a global scale allows us to begin to measure the scale of personal and generational traumas that are still present among us. Through this process, we are better able to understand our individual and collective experiences as we develop more awareness, tools for interpretation, and ultimately, for transformation.

Erasing language and knowledge has always been a crucial part of rewriting history and culture to favor the powerful, hence the repeated historical pattern of burning libraries, banning books and languages, and blocking access to information. Conversely, truth-telling through knowledge and language recovery is a sacred practice of resistance and an effective strategy for recovering our own historical truths, cultural narratives and identities.

As we learn how to recognize the ways in which the dominating language practices of conquest and colonization have become embedded in how we understand our past, we can better understand how it is currently being used against us and actively work to replace those narratives with truer ones.

There are scores of examples to illustrate this, but let's take a look at two:

A domestic example can be found in the forced displacement of tens of thousands of Indigenous people of the Five Tribes (Choctaw, Cherokee, Muscogee (Creek), Chickasaw, and Seminole) and enslaved African and African American people from their homes and lands in the US South to Indian reservations west of Mississippi River through the Indian Removal Act of 1830. Though commonly known as the "Trail of Tears," when it is used outside of its original language and indigenous cultural context and worldview, this flowery language can diminish the scale of the historical reality in which the then-president of the United States, Andrew Jackson, ordered the forced relocation of entire peoples to encourage Western Expansion and steal 25 million acres of land for white settlement. This was not a rogue act by a single man with power; it was a law that was first passed by the United States Congress, and then the death march was carried out by the US military. It was a horrific act of ethnic cleansing that murdered thousands upon thousands of women, men, and children—old and young alike—on US soil by the government of the United States of America less than 200 years ago.

An international example from global economics is the use of binary labels like "underdeveloped" versus "developed" nations or "First World" versus "Third World" nations. These language frameworks assign value to nations in the Global North while simultaneously erasing the colonial past that originally created and continue to perpetuate the unequal economic relationships between countries. More historically accurate descriptors such as "colonizing" and "colonized" nations would more accurately identify the antagonistic nations who perpetuate domination and benefit from the spoils of invasion, pillage, war, and exploitation of foreign people and lands.[16]

As long as we remain unaware of the historical and political realities that have shaped our moral and cultural values, we are more easily convinced that the state of injustice and violence in the world today is inevitable, and the natural consequence of personal sin and divine order. This opens the way for us to be manipulated into submitting to the expectations and control of others, particularly when it comes under the guise of faith.

white Christian Supremacy is the origin and underlying context of Spiritual Violence because it provides the ideological frameworks that justify harm to certain people deemed less worthy of safety, equality, and abundant life. Spiritual Trauma is the consequence of Spiritual Violence (including its extreme forms, Spiritual Terrorism and Religious Abuse), yet all these can be traced back to the ideologies of white Christian Supremacy that enable them.

Now that we have examined some of the historical realities of white Christian Supremacy along with its arrival to this hemisphere, the following chapters will focus on the concepts of Spiritual Violence.

3: Spiritual Violence

Spiritual Violence occurs whenever religious morality or divine authority is used to question or deny the sacred worth and inherent dignity of a person or group. It can happen in any social context by any person, group or institution. It is based on the social and religious ideologies of white Christian Supremacy, and it can produce emotional, psychological, and spiritual wounds even when enacted unintentionally or by a close friend, partner, or family member.

By teasing out the pieces of faith that are rooted in legacies of colonization and white Christian Supremacy, we can identify Spiritual Violence for what it is—violence—rather than believing it is something holy. Regardless of faith tradition, white Christian Supremacy impacts every single body that inhabits lands colonized by the imperial forces that used religion to justify violence and exploitation. Not only because its legacies are the nefarious foundations of our societies, but also because many forms of Christianity continue to work in the service of those who weaponize it for power or control.

Spiritual Violence is the misuse of the power of spirituality—in this case Christianity—as a weapon to diminish or negate the human dignity of a person or group of people. Its destructive force appropriates religious ideologies to inflict emotional, psychological, and/or spiritual injury. It occurs any time "God," the Bible, or religion-based morality causes harm—whether intentional or not. From the most ordinary daily interactions to full-on structural violence against entire communities, Spiritual Violence pervades every layer of our social fabric. It can be something as unassuming as a negative comment or joke, or as serious as a hate crime, femicide, or systematic criminalization of a group of people.

Just as no one is immune to being harmed by Spiritual Violence, no one is exempt from participating in it. Because white Christian Supremacy permeates our perceptions of right and wrong, Spiritual Violence can be enacted by anyone and in any social context. It is easy to recognize malice when the attack comes from a stranger shouting slurs about what we look like, who we are with, or how we are expressing ourselves. Unfortunately, some of the deepest wounds of Spiritual Violence can come from interactions with those with whom we have loving personal relationships.

When people who are close to us offer "constructive criticism" about things we cannot change about ourselves, they likely do so with good intentions. Many are sincerely convinced that their advice is "for our own good," and that they want us to change because they love us. This noble intention, though, does not change the impacts of their words and actions. In these situations, it is likely that the person hurting us is repeating the same messages and acting on the same beliefs that they have received—ideas that originate in white Christian Supremacy.

SENTIPENSAR: FEELING OUT OF PLACE

There are times in which our most authentic selves feel safe, affirmed, and celebrated either in a community or with particular people. Unfortunately, there are also moments in which we realize that some parts of ourselves are different, and some previously welcoming spaces and people have become a barrier to our most authentic self-expression. When we sense that some piece of our identity is being demeaned or excluded, we may suddenly feel "out of place" or fearful of fully expressing ourselves freely.

It is important to note that this fear is often a result of Spiritual Violence and not a sign that something is wrong with us. If you have ever gone through this, take a moment to acknowledge the feelings associated with these experiences and attend to wherever these emotions and memories have settled into your body. If working with others, share an affirmation about the personal worth of each member of the group or write an affirmation for yourself.

Those of us who have centered spirituality as a core part of our lives at one time or another have an especially intimate relationship with Spiritual Violence, because religion has molded and held our deepest longings, hopes, and vulnerabilities. Our faith is or has been a deeply personal source of guidance in the ways we understand the world and the people around us, as well as ourselves and our place in community.

When we are embraced and nurtured by others in the faith, it is life-giving. But for those of us who have dared to ask the difficult questions, point out hypocrisy within the church, question religious authorities, commit a sin deemed unforgivable, or who have walked away from a religious space where we no longer feel like we belong, the opposite is equally true. Losing a community of faith where we once felt at home can be devastating. It can lead to questioning our sense of self. It can disconnect us from our spirituality, and even distance us from our own souls.

On both a family and a community level, Spiritual Violence regularly appears in the form of blatant and subtle threats of rejection or punishment. This can show up in many forms, from negative comments, jokes, or looks of disapproval to explicit verbal condemnation or physical punishment for something like how we express our gender or live into our sexuality.

Especially when there is an imbalance of power due to family dynamics, economic interdependence, or differences in age, gender, health, ability, etc., we can easily feel trapped and forced to live within established norms for safety, survival, and belonging. As a result, we deny ourselves the full exploration of our own identities and desires and often hide our true selves away to avoid spiritual and physical harm, all of which are reasonable natural responses to very real danger.

In addition to the explicit messages we receive, we also respond to implicit messaging by telling ourselves that we need to turn off those parts of ourselves that make us different in order to be accepted and loved. Thus, even when there isn't an immediate danger to our physical bodies, there is a kind of brutality in Spiritual Violence that cuts deep into the psyche and leaves long-lasting wounds that are difficult to heal.

JELENA

Jelena is a proud *cimarronaje*, the great-granddaughter of enslaved people who escaped their bondage to live free on the island. She was born in the *Período especial*, the economic crisis of 1990s in Cuba, after the Soviet Union fell. Food was scarce and long blackouts were common, but she found great comfort in spending Sundays worshipping alongside her extended family late into the evenings. She eventually found her place in their small congregation as a musician.

Unlike most mainline churches in Cuba who inherited the white supremacist and capitalist legacy of North American missionaries, Jelena's community was filled with *afrodescendiente* people like her who taught her that Jesus was a revolutionary, a rebel who fought against injustice and who had a preference for the poor and oppressed. Yet even in her own family, the traditional gender expectations and the colonial values of patriarchy reigned supreme. She learned that a "good" woman is a submissive wife that dedicates her life to caring for her home, her husband, and their children.

Jelena already knew at a young age that she did not want to fulfill those gender roles, and she hated every dress and skirt she was ever made to wear. Though she never spoke of these things out loud, she often wondered if she could still be "good" in the sight of the Lord (and her family) without them. Once, when she was only six years old, Jelena had an experience with her older sister that would stay with her for the rest of her life.

During an especially long blackout, her family gathered around the dining table, lit the candles they had left, and began to pray. Jelena's older sister –who was almost 15 and very much her role model– prayed jokingly, "Dear God, please please please, let me not be a *negra* [Black] or a *tortillera* [dyke]!" Everyone around the table laughed. Jelena didn't know what a "tortillera" was, but she did know that they were definitely *negra*, and she didn't understand why it was funny. It was a small joke that had big emotional implications for her. Beneath the laughter flowed potent values about identity and worth. It was the day that Jelena began to recognize that there was something very wrong with being in the skin she was in.

Years later, when Jelena fell in love for the first time, her sister's laughter echoed in her head. Jelena loved spending time with Cindy, who had been her friend at school, her playmate on the playground and around the neighborhood, and they had even gone to the same church for a while. They had known each other for years, but when they started a romantic relationship, Cindy's father saw how often they were together and began making disparaging comments about Jelena's hair, skin color, and character traits. "She looks like a homosexual. You shouldn't be hanging out with people like that; people will think you are one of those people." Then randomly one day, he told his daughter, "I mean, I'm not racist...We can have Black friends, but at a distance." When Cindy confessed why she wasn't allowed to spend time with her anymore, Jelena's heart dropped. Once again, she was reminded of her two unforgivable sins: being Black and a *tortillera*.

These kinds of violences, both microaggressions and outright discrimination, made Jelena feel like an outsider, not only at college and in her workplace, but even in her own family. Every assault on a part of her humanity felt like it slowly drained her dignity and chipped away at her soul. Things got much worse as her country got embroiled in the same-sex marriage debate. Catholic and evangelical churches banded together to fight for a one-woman, one-man definition of marriage in the new constitution. At church, she began to feel like an imposter, as if even her prayers were tainted with the deceit of what she was. She was shocked at the hate and condemnation in her own church, her own family; gay people were equated to pedophiles and criminals. She often thought, *Are these not the very people who taught me about unconditional love, and how Jesus requires us to love one another? Do they not know the impact of their words?* It was no wonder to Jelena why so many of her gay friends felt like life was unlivable...she herself felt like she couldn't go on at times.

She was so fed up with living a double life, that one Saturday she went to a PRIDE march and rally in Havana, more out of frustration than courage. Even though she was scared, she felt more joy, more peace, and more at home than she had in years. The chants in the streets and speakers in the park helped her begin to connect the dots between her own intersectional identities and the experiences of others. She not only found community, but she also found language: words and concepts to identify things she had felt, but didn't have a way to explain: homophobia, racism, misogyny, white supremacy, cultural genocide, intersectionality, systems of oppression.

Since then, Jelena has learned to love her Queer Black

flesh, her curvy body and her Afro hair that crowns her head, symbolizing Mother Africa who lives within her. She finds her ancestors all around her in daily life; she is now able to recognize how many of her family's customs are actually rooted in the cultural practices and religious beliefs of her African ancestors, even though her entire family is devoutly Christian.

Jelena's androgynous style and iconic rainbow bracelet often announce her identity even before she speaks. She is an advocate for the LGBTQ community, though she still longs for a space where she can live out her spirituality. She often wonders, *How can this religion with its white, cisgender, colonial Jesus be relevant, liberating, and empowering for a Black, Latina, lesbian woman? Does this heteronormative, adult-centric faith have anything to offer so many diverse young people who are in search of a spiritual home and full, abundant life? Can it help those of us trying to make a world where everyone has a place to be safe and be loved?*

The Spiritual Violence of Patriarchy

Since homophobia and transphobia are rooted in misogyny, understanding the Spiritual Violence perpetuated by sexism illuminates the inherent gender-based violence of physical, legal, emotional/psychological, cultural, and spiritual attacks on LGBTQIA+ people. Patriarchy is often described as the social system that privileges men over women. In and of itself, this is spiritually violent, because it tries to thwart the fundamental truth that all human beings are of equal worth and are entitled to human rights and dignity.

One of the central reasons patriarchy continues to persist is because religion is used to perpetuate the prevailing Christian belief that it is the natural order of society set in place by God. The ideologies of white Christian Supremacy depend on extensive networks of circular logic and binary thinking to sustain its claims about power and God. These create hierarchies that organize everything including which people are more or less deserving of rights and advantages in society. Sex is only one of the many assigned categories; others include race, gender expression, sexual orientation, religion, age, ability, class, citizenship, language, education, ethnicity, familial status, etc.

In a world that is already oriented toward hierarchical structures, attributing male dominance or any other privileged identity to God's design and calling it the natural order of the universe is an effective strategy. We have been taught in deed, if not also in words, that patriarchy is the form of human leadership and control that God created, when in fact, it is a human invention that gets projected onto God to justify its existence. God, as the ultimate authority, is commandeered to serve patriarchal systems of dominance and make them more powerful and harder to contest.

Sometimes it is difficult to identify all the ways God has been deployed to create social stratification. For example, within patriarchy, all masculinities are not valued equally. Some are not acknowledged at all. Cisheteropatriarchy is a term that visibilizes the particular forms of gender-based violence perpetrated against the LGBTQIA+ community because of the kind of masculinity that is privileged in our present-day societies, namely cisgendered, heterosexual dominant masculinity.

From this vantage point, those in positions of authority use reverse logic to justify their claims to power through divine right and blessing. However, the reality is that the foundations of modern-day societies in this hemisphere have been constructed to replicate the worldview of the elite European colonizers who imposed their system of racist logic and imperialist morality. An example of white Christian Supremacist logic within patriarchy can be laid out in the following way:

> Men hold positions of power and authority at every level of society, from government to families. God, the Creator of everything, must have put men in these positions of power because men are stronger, smarter, and built for leadership. And if God, himself, is masculine, and his son, Jesus, came to earth as a man, then certainly God favors masculinity, and men must be superior to women. And if masculinity is intrinsically better suited for leadership, then patriarchy is the natural, God-intended order of things. Therefore, we should not only submit to our place in the hierarchy, but we should actively oppose anything

> that threatens it, such as feminism. And, as needed, the Bible can prove that this is true.

Accordingly, one could generate a similar logic model for any other identity that white Christian Supremacy prioritizes such as white, Christian, able-bodied, English-speaking, US citizen, adult, person with wealth, etc. This strategy of deception has been so successful that most people simply accept it as true. Gone unquestioned, this creates a dangerous power dynamic that ripples out into all of society.

For example, if we believe that God created two (and only two) diametrically opposed sexes—each with its own essential and complementary purpose, each with his or her distinct anatomical and physiological reality, emotional and intellectual capacity, and leadership potential, then fulfilling gender expectations of the sex that has been assigned to us feels like a divine mandate and part of our religious duty as Christians.

Thus, it is no coincidence that the gender a person is given at birth impacts almost every aspect of our lives. From toys we are given, to the emotions we are allowed to show, to the color and style of clothes we should wear, the expectations for how we are to express our gender is made clear from the earliest moments of life. Career possibilities, personal grooming habits, hobbies, food preferences, beauty standards, sexual practices, and especially, with whom one should fall in love and create a family are all ascribed to a person based on our visible genitalia at birth. In this way, patriarchy harms everyone by restricting how and who we can be—even cisgender, heterosexual men, who are at the top of the patriarchal food chain. Every single life is negatively affected by these gendered social pressures and their corresponding institutional limitations.

To disregard a person's natural affinities and mandate them to submission or dominance based on perceived anatomy at birth is gender-based violence. To sacrifice a person's human rights in order to prop up a socio-political system grounded in inequality is morally wrong. To claim that patriarchy is the natural order of Creation in which each person has an inescapable, intrinsic essence as a man or a woman based solely on whether one has a penis or vagina is a systemic attack on the innate worth of every person, either through internalized oppression or internalized privilege. To do all of this under the guise of religious authority in the name of God, is Spiritual Violence.

Even when we believe in the pre-scripted ideals of white Christian Supremacy and aspire to live into them, there are ways in which we simply cannot comply with all the expectations of every single one of the many identities we each carry in our bodies. When we do not fulfill the roles assigned to us by systems of power, there are real consequences.

Let's reflect on the following narrative as a lived example of how this plays out in real life:

SOFIA

Sofia has always been the baby in a middle-class Catholic family. She lived a happy childhood in the suburbs where she was always surrounded by family and friends. It was a big decision to leave home and go away to college, but she quickly found a community in a campus youth ministry that focused on after-school activities and summer camp for underprivileged children. She loved sharing Jesus' message of love for all people, especially to those who hadn't received as many blessings and opportunities as she had.

On one of their weekend retreats, Sofia started developing feelings for one of the guys in the group who was another summer camp counselor, and they soon started dating. Alex was the sweetest guy she had ever met. He was amazing with the kids, always so patient and easy going. He was quiet, thoughtful and kind, and importantly, he never pressured her sexually. Sometimes they would just walk around holding hands and talking about their faith for hours. It felt so right, like a fairytale! It didn't take long before Sofia was head over heels in love and often wondered if Alex could be "the one" that God had sent especially for her.

As winter break approached, Sofia wanted to invite Alex home with her to meet her family. She couldn't contain her excitement as she told him about all about the things they could do in her hometown, visiting her home church, the lake where they could go swimming in the summer, and all the people she wanted him to meet.

Alex didn't respond the way she expected; he got stone still and wouldn't meet her eyes. She had no idea what was going on, and she felt like she wanted to burst into tears, but she just stayed quiet and waited. Alex took a deep breath and asked if they could take a walk. They were quiet for a long time. Sofia was sure he was going to break up with her, and just as she started to break the silence, Alex whispered, "I wasn't born a boy." Sofia was in shock; confusion, surprise, and terror swept over her. He continued, "I wanted to tell you before this goes any deeper. I'm already in love with you, and if you can't accept me, I need to know now, before I meet your family and everything else that goes with it."

Over the next few hours, Alex shared his testimony of

how God had saved his life. Alex told her about his experiences as a child when he was obsessed with dying; how he fought his parents when they tried to put him dresses; how he always wanted his hair short and how his parents finally had to shave it all off when he took a pair of kitchen scissors and cut clumps of hair to the scalp at five years old. His parents were worried about him all the time; sometimes he heard his mother crying when she prayed at night. They tried their best to love him and let him be himself, except at church where he still had to wear a dress, and everyone called him by a girl's name. Sofia hardly said a word, but somewhere along the way their pace slowed, and she found her hand in his.

The worst had started when Alex began menstruating. His mom freaked out when she found him binding his chest with ace bandages from the medicine cabinet. Alex told her about the hours and hours of spiritual guidance he sat through with the pastor each week, and the special church camp where his parents had sent him because they promised to cure their daughter. Sofia held her breath as he spoke the horrors of that place. She couldn't fathom such things happening to anyone, much less in the name of Jesus.

"Did you ever talk to a doctor?" she asked quietly. He nodded, but he kept his head down, ashamed. "Everything changed when I came back from that camp. My parents were so disappointed, and I was traumatized. I knew there was no fixing me, and I just wanted it all to end." Sofia couldn't stop the tears as Alex talked about being hospitalized after his last suicide attempt. He had gotten pretty close and felt like it was only by the grace of God that he had survived it. She couldn't imagine a world without him.

"After that, everything changed –slowly– but we all knew something had to give. God sent many angels to us during that time." It was the first time he had spoken with a counselor who wasn't part of the church, and his parents were so scared and desperate they were willing to try anything. That was when he began to transition. They changed churches, and he changed schools and started going by "Alex" full-time. He explained to her how he was allowed to start hormone therapy at 16, which is why he had facial hair and looked pretty normal, with one exception. Alex had had top surgery the summer he turned 18, and the scars were still very visible. Sofia asked to see, and he slowly lifted his shirt. She gasped at the scars cutting across his chest, but she was even more surprised at herself when she reached out to touch Alex's chest and immediately thought of Christ showing his scars to his disciples after his resurrection.

"I know it's a lot. I understand if you don't want to date a Trans guy. I'm sorry I didn't tell you before now...I just didn't know how. I haven't felt this much for someone before...and I didn't want to ruin it. This is who I am, and I am happy, but I don't want to keep any secrets from you." They hugged for a long time, and Sofia asked for time to process everything she had just heard.

She couldn't sleep that night, her thoughts vacillating between what Alex had gone through, and her own fear, anger, and confusion. She didn't know if she was allowed to pray about it, but God felt like the only one she could talk to...She loved Alex, but...*he was born a girl, so did that mean she was a lesbian? She had found friends and community in the youth ministry, but what if the others found out? Would Alex be kicked out...would she be an outcast too? She felt so happy with Alex; she loved how they prayed together and how she felt totally at ease with him...but could she keep his secret? What would her family say if they found out...when they found out? Oh God, and sex!* She hadn't even thought about that...it was too much to wrap her mind around.

Once upon a time she had dreamed of becoming a missionary in a foreign land when she grew up, and though that had seemed impossibly hard, it felt like an easier path than the completely unknown one before her now.

Misogyny is the set of cultural practices that enforce patriarchal norms and expectations, rewarding those who follow their prescribed gender identity and punishing those who break the rules. Embedded ideologies of white Christian Supremacy sanction the policing of bodies as holy and salvific in an evil, "fallen" world.

Misogyny regularly weaponizes Christian morality for social control. It creates structures in which anyone who does not fit neatly into their prescribed gender—from how they dress, to who they love, to the profession they choose—faces unnecessary challenges that are legitimized as the obvious consequence of being sinful and going against the will of God. Real concrete repercussions, from isolation to violence, are often not far behind.

Patriarchal narratives claim that men are more like God and therefore more valuable to God, a moral justification that feminists reject as untrue and unjust. In response, we are told that under patriarchy women are in fact equal and as valuable as men, we just have a different purpose and function. Yet the lived experiences of women tell of a different reality. From sexual violence to unequal pay for equal work, from the dangerous conditions and limited care around pregnancy and reproduction to invisible unpaid domestic labor, separate but equal does not work out well for most women and girls, both in society and in church.

Challenging the culture of patriarchy means confronting the ongoing legacies of the religion of colonization and settler colonialism that set it in place. white Christian Supremacy would have us believe that the gendered power dynamics of patriarchy simply replicate the relationship between God and humanity. Theologically, this is not only detrimental to women, but an attack on God. Thus, the battle for how we understand God and the characteristics we associate with that God are vitally important. These conclusions either limit or expand the communal imagination of a society.

Patriarchy has created a god in its own image—all-powerful, egocentric, violent, independent, controlling, and male. His roles are ones of traditional patriarchy: father, judge, warrior, king. Patriarchy has stolen the theological language, traditions, and sacred text of Christianity to falsify the proof of its claims.

The Bible is used to proof-text misogyny by those who benefit from it, as well as by those who have been indoctrinated to submit to it as a spiritual and moral obligation. For systems of power and domination, proof-texting is an intentional premeditated tactic. It is no mistake that most images of Christ traditionally paint him as an attractive white man with light hair and blue eyes, even though this is a projection of what white Christian Supremacy wants Jesus to look like, not what he was.

For those of us who are combating patriarchy or trying to reclaim our faith, the decision to read the Bible through a more liberative approach has to be just as deliberate. The biblical text in Genesis can and has been used to make Eve responsible for the Fall of Creation in the Garden of Eden. It can and has been used to justify the claim that women should be meek and are commanded to be submissive to men. However, it can also be used to prove the exact opposite.

The first creation story in Genesis can be used to assert that people of all genders were created equal and at the same time.[17] The Bible can demonstrate how women can be excellent religious and political leaders who should be respected and obeyed.[18] It also tells stories of people who did not fit into the male-female gender binary.[19] Even more radical is the sound theological reasoning that makes the claim that Jesus is Trans.[20]

Just as the sacred text gives examples of a patriarchal God with the traits of toxic masculinity, it also contains images of God in feminine form.[21] Additionally, God is often referred to in plural form, providing legitimate justification for using they and them pronouns when referring to God.[22] These are but a few examples of how renewed approaches to the text are possible if we are willing to expand our hearts, decolonize our minds, and open our imaginations to a living Word.

Turning the Violence Inward

Over time, we take the poisonous lies of white Christian Supremacy into our bodies and spirits as we are constantly bombarded with its im/moral frameworks. Internalization is the process of accepting these negative ideas about ourselves and taking them to heart such that we truly believe there is something wrong with us. That belief then becomes our guiding force. Once we are convinced that certain fundamental aspects of our identity are inferior, unnatural, sinful, sick, or evil, we perpetuate the Spiritual Violence of white Christian Supremacy within ourselves where it becomes inescapable.

As a result of believing that parts of ourselves must be cut away, changed, hidden, or ignored, we may attempt, with varying degrees of success, to extinguish or repress these aspects of our authentic personhood. Eventually, external reinforcement is no longer needed as we will continue to surveil ourselves and police our own self-expression as long as we believe there truly is something bad about who we are.

Consequently, we may experience depression, anxiety, and cycles of grief, anger, and frustration. Others of us may feel numb or distant from our own body and reality. And still others will choose a route of escape where we understand everything we experience as reinforcement that confirms what we already believe about ourselves. This is called confirmation bias. Here, we interpret all information and feedback in a way that supports our belief that we deserve to be punished, creating a modern-day self-flagellation.

Common responses to internalized Spiritual Violence also include numbing and self-medicating with substances (alcohol, drugs, etc.), inflicting harm on ourselves or others, pushing our bodies to physical extremes, and escaping through entertainment or social media.

Even though Scripture dwells on the commandments of loving our neighbors and caring for those in need, logics of white Christian Supremacy condition us to judge others and ourselves with a presumption of sinfulness and guilt. This encourages apathy towards others' suffering as well as our own. Common refrains that desensitize us sound like: "They had it coming." Or "That's such a shame, but it's just the way things are." Or "Well… what can you really do about it?" At scale, social injustices and systemic violence are assumed to be a consequence of God's judgement and punishment rather than a reflection of society's supremacist culture of cruelty.

Many harmful ideas are so normalized that they cease to be interrogated, such as the belief that some people are inherently bad or slightly inferior. Historically, People of Color, immigrants, people with disabilities, poor people, and anyone who steps out of line with the status quo fall into this logic of white Christian Supremacy. It follows then that whatever discrimination or violence comes to us is deserved, or at the very least, that others' problems are none of our concern or responsibility.

This is especially true on the individual level, such that, if something bad happens, the most common response is that the victim must have done something wrong to deserve it. We often repeat these narratives to ourselves as well. Negative self-talk, self-exclusion, and self-harm are prevalent expressions of internalized Spiritual Violence.

No one is exempt from perpetuating these logics of white Christian Supremacy. Even for those of us with marginalized identities, we commonly reproduce these forms of violence against other marginalized communities, our own communities, and most often, ourselves. For example, many Christians harbor a fear that God is behind the bad things that happen to us or our loved ones, secretly believing that we are being punished for some past thought or action. The idea of the Divine as a strict overlord—always at the ready to mete out pain and allow suffering as punishment for our failures and shortcomings—is so common in many religious communities that the fear of God's wrath often overshadows the image of a loving God that responds to us with compassion and understanding.

Identifying our lived realities, speaking honestly about our internal narratives, and becoming familiar with their impacts in our lives begins the process of understanding the breadth and depth of Spiritual Violence at play in our internal world. From there, it becomes easier to step out from under the weight of guilt, fear, and shame that comes along with not living into the expectations set out for us from birth. In that process, we create more space to reclaim our own authentic identity and spirituality.

SENTIPENSAR: TENSION RELEASE BODY PRACTICE

The enduring legacy of white Christian Supremacy can be traced to this very moment; its fingerprints mark each of our bodies through the Spiritual Violence we've endured. As we decode these indelible and pervasive messages, we begin to recognize how they control everything from how we move our bodies, to how to sit, how to dress, and how to relate to others' bodies.

Even though we cannot change the ways that white Christian Supremacy marks history, we can begin to examine and reclaim the intimate terrain of our own embodiment. The following movement practice is an example of a simple exercise that can be done individually or in a group whenever needed to recenter in our bodies in the present moment.

With soft music on in the background, lay down on your back and consciously let go of the weight of your body while you listen to the music. To relax more deeply, try tensing up your whole body for a few seconds and then release while you exhale slowly. Once you are in sync to the rhythm of your breathing, begin gently shaking your body. Start with your feet, and then let the movement rise slowly into your calves, your thighs, hips, back, torso, arms, hands, neck, and head. Intensify the shaking as it moves up your body. After a few seconds of shaking, pause and rest for a moment, listening to the music and letting the weight of your body sink into the surface beneath you.

Repeat this exercise two or three times—a bit of shaking and then a moment of stillness. This will help you to become more conscious of the memories your body carries while simultaneously allowing you to release tension and give yourself a sense of calm and tranquility. You can also do this exercise standing up if your space is limited.

Weaponizing the Word

The Bible is referred to as the "Sword of the Spirit," but more often, it has been used as a weapon of Spiritual Violence. Biblical Literalism is the belief among some Christians that the Bible is literally words that God spoke that were written down by human scribes without error or differences of opinion on how to translate or interpret them. By reading the Bible in this way, it becomes an effective tool of social control.[23]

When sacred texts are categorized as infallible, power is consolidated in those who have the authority to decipher and interpret the text. It forecloses the opportunity to engage the text, discern its meanings for oneself, or question authority—either that of the text, the leader, or institution with the power to control its content. It also shuts out additional outside wisdom that might contradict or color the text such as contributions from the fields of archeology, world history, comparative religion, and ancient literature to name a few possibilities.

Biblical Literalism also ignores the reality that there are no existing copies of the original texts, and that there are thousands of interpretations and translations of the more than 30,000 verses of the Bible. Its narratives are often taken out of their historical contexts, translated and adapted erroneously—with or without any intention to distort the Scripture. Consequently, we receive these interpretations as though they were irrefutable proof of God's sanctioning.

Regardless of one's personal investment in the Bible as a guidebook for right and wrong, Christian morality culturally impacts everyone through the foundational structures and institutions of society on which it is built. For example, our legal system is entirely constructed around the sensibilities and logics of white Christian Supremacy pretending to be an altruistic and benevolent religion.

Let's take sodomy laws as a case study to illustrate this point:

Laws prohibiting homosexuality are historically called "sodomy laws," taken from an erroneous interpretation of the Sodom and Gomorrah narrative in the book of Genesis. The word "homosexuality" did not even appear in the Bible until 1946.[24] And even though biblical scholars and religious leaders have long since demonstrated that this narrative has nothing to do with Queer desire or consensual homosexual sex,[25] it is still used in Christian countries all over the world to outlaw same-sex sexual relations and endanger the lives of countless innocent LGBTQIA+ people.

When prosecuted under these laws, Queer and Trans people are accused of "crimes against nature" based on the white Christian Supremacist claim that God only created human beings as heterosexual and cisgender. This myth persists even with extensive undisputed evidence that the biology, anatomy, and chemistry of gender expression and sexual orientation are incredibly complex and vary widely across all of Creation. Nevertheless, LGBTQIA+ people are labeled "unnatural" by society and by the State even with irrefutable research and observation that homosexuality and bisexuality are completely normal in the natural world, documented in more than 1,500 animal species—including mammals like humans.[26]

In this example of sexuality and gender, the Bible could equally be used to support equal human rights and dignity for everyone, even when approaching the text through a literalist lens. However, the ideologies of white Christian Supremacy tend toward weaponizing the text rather than using it as a tool of liberation. Some of the most spiritually violent rhetoric begins when people use the Bible—literally called the "Word of God"—to empower themselves to speak on behalf of the Divine and pass judgement on others by invoking the authority of the most supreme being in the universe. It is no coincidence then, which topics come up time and again: personal sin and culpability, submission and obedience to authority, holy sacrifice and suffering, and inevitably, God's judgment. Each holds the eternal promise of Heaven as reward or Hell as punishment that can be effectively leveraged for control and Spiritual Violence.

Most of us who seek spiritual wisdom in the biblical text do so for guidance and to develop a closer relationship with God. We want to be good and do right. We do not often recognize the ways in which white Christian Supremacy has primed us to receive certain messages that reinforce what we expect to find in the text. We are preconditioned to accept stories in which God is a jealous and destructive tyrant; where women are praised almost exclusively for their maternity and obedience; and where heteropatriarchy is strictly enforced and celebrated as virtuous. These are repeated and mirrored back in real life so often that they become "common sense" for most people in Christian societies even though there are ample counter narratives within the same biblical canon to dispute them.

Typically, we do not question whether the Bible actually says the things we are told, because we are so prepared to receive the messages of white Christian Supremacy pre-installed in our societies since colonization. It can be painful to recognize our place within these violent and repressive religious ideologies in which some people are considered chosen by God to dominate and rule while everyone else is forced to silently acquiesce. For some believers, this realization is a breaking point. For others, it can serve as motivation to delve deeper into the faith in all its aspects and learn more about alternative Christian theologies and biblical interpretations. Either way, there comes a point in which the veil of naiveté is removed, and the truth of our own complicity is no longer invisible to us.

SENTIPENSAR: FEELING THE QUESTIONS

It can be difficult for Christians to come to terms with the reality that the Bible has been used to inflict such harm and religion-based violence when we have received so many important, formative lessons and encouragement from the same texts we consider sacred. This tension can be uncomfortable, and it can give rise to a variety of emotions and reactions including fear and resistance to the facts. Many people experience feelings of anger, hurt, and betrayal when we learn the truth about the historical and lived realities of the Bible. We can feel deceived and misled into believing that the Bible was a perfect, infallible text, synonymous with the literal "Word of God."

Spend a few minutes writing out your questions about the Bible that have come up for you. Then freewrite how you feel and your emotional response to those questions. It is not necessary to analyze the questions, your reactions, or to interrogate your emotions. For today, it is enough to note them and recognize that they are a part of the healing process.

Recognizing Spiritual Violence in Daily Life

Identifying as a survivor and perpetrator of Spiritual Violence and an heir to a colonizing Christianity that has caused harm to ourselves and others is a difficult, yet powerful, first step toward healing and spiritual reclamation. The more we know about Spiritual Violence, the better prepared we are to identify and interrupt it as it occurs in daily life all around us. Though it is impossible to ensure that Spiritual Violence will never happen, we can create effective strategies for protection against the impacts it has on our bodies and our lives.

Spiritual Violence is at work any time a person or a group of people use sacred texts, doctrines, or religious traditions to claim moral superiority, and therefore authority, over others' lives and experiences. Whether as part of a government, an institution, a group, or as an individual, those who utilize the tactics of Spiritual Violence do so because they feel authorized and empowered to make value judgments about others, and that almost always leads to violence or the threat of harm in one form or another.

Much of the Spiritual Violence we encounter growing up is so commonplace that it may seem normal. Experiences that are deeply embedded in our family dynamics and cultural norms can be even more difficult to identify as harmful. Even if we feel pain when they happen, we perceive them as well-established patterns that cannot be changed. As a result, experiences of Spiritual Violence may feel confusing or difficult to name for those of us who have lived through them in our daily lives.

To better understand Spiritual Violence in practice, we have included a Reflective Awareness Tool in Appendix 1 to explore commonly occurring examples of how Spiritual Violence is deployed. These include painful interpersonal interactions, internalized messages about our goodness and worthiness, as well as impositions of patriarchy, heteronormativity, and other power imbalances. Even in subtle ways, the unholy union of religion and power filters down into the most intimate spheres of our daily lives.

From the widest scope at the level of society to the most intimate and personal purview of an individual life, Spiritual Violence leaves painful wounds that can be challenging to heal. Its impacts on our physical, emotional, and spiritual wellbeing can range from mild to life-threatening. Appendix 2 offers some practical strategies for where to start in the healing process. It is not always easy to see ourselves as survivors of Spiritual Violence, or as perpetrators of the same, or as both at once, but understanding our lived experiences with Spiritual Violence is necessary in our work of healing and spiritual reclamation.

As a broad and pervasive religious phenomenon, Spiritual Violence manifests at every level of influence with varying degrees of violence and harm. Now that we have covered the basics of Spiritual Violence, we will go deeper into two extreme manifestations of it: Spiritual Terrorism in Chapter 4 and Religious Abuse in Chapter 5. The common denominator between these is the abuse of the spiritual power that comes with invoking the name of God, the symbols, sacred texts, or culture of Christianity in order to diminish, condemn, or attack the sacred worth and/or physical well-being of a person or group of people.

4: Spiritual Terrorism

Spiritual Violence can escalate beyond the individual or interpersonal spheres to mold and influence entire societies. Spiritual Violence intensifies into Spiritual Terrorism when the binary logic of white Christian Supremacy reduces people and whole communities into overly simplistic categories of "good or bad," and creates a "for us or against us" mentality. Moral arguments based in white Christian Supremacy are then used as the foundation for discrimination, unjust laws, and exacerbated social stigma.

Ongoing threats of violence and punishment seek to control social behavior and resources. If ignored or contested, those in power feel justified using military and law enforcement as mechanisms for repression and punishment against those who do not submit to their impositions. Spiritual Terrorism describes the full-on assault at a systemic level against those with the identities and characteristics deemed dangerous and evil, and it coerces subjugation by intentionally destroying any sense of safety for targeted groups.

Spiritual Terrorism can be differentiated from Spiritual Violence in three primary ways: scale, scope, and intensity. Both deploy corrupt morality and the authority of God to achieve its ends, but Spiritual Terrorism occurs at a larger scale, has a wider reach, and a more aggressive malicious intent. It puts certain peoples' lives under a microscope with constant surveillance and judgement under the assumption that their marginalized identity makes them immoral and criminal.

First, the scale Spiritual Terrorism is created through threats and acts of violence at a system-wide and institutional level for anyone who exhibits the targeted identity. It is not specific to one person or one particular place or institution (unless they are being made an example for the rest of the community); it targets all people with a specific identity marker, such as race, gender, immigration status, religion, sexual orientation, etc. and deliberately condemns, excludes, and systematically terrorizes applicable individuals and communities.

Second, the scope of reach with Spiritual Terrorism is vast and comprehensive. It intentionally torments targeted individuals and communities from multiple centers of power at once. Spiritual Terrorism is violently enforced at every level of society from enforcement of discriminatory laws and policies down to the interpersonal level through social groups and institutions. It purposely tries to remove access to spaces that traditionally understand themselves to be safe havens for all, such as schools, libraries, churches, and even families. It instead turns them into hostile and dangerous spaces for the targeted group.

On the receiving end, Spiritual Terrorism is designed to feel suffocating and inescapable. It nullifies basic universal human rights to safety, peace, and wellbeing, among others. People experiencing Spiritual Terrorism feel the constant threat of judgement, repression, violence, and the elimination of their rights and dignity with no way out other than to subdue the identity being targeted to the extent possible.

Lastly, there is a status change that moves a group of people over the threshold from being targets of Spiritual Violence into victims of Spiritual Terrorism. It occurs when a specific identity marker goes from simply being undesirable to being publicly branded as evil and an enemy of civilized society. There is an instigated shift in the wider communal imaginary about those who carry these traits—from being passively disliked to being actively hunted down because they pose a dangerous threat that must be quelled or eliminated.

Those in positions of moral authority and institutional power—politicians, police officers, faith leaders, etc.—who create the dehumanizing narratives and oversee these conditions of terror, often feel justified in their aggressions because of the false moral claim that they represent the "good guys" while those with the targeted identity marker are "the enemy."

Thus, Spiritual Terrorism can be defined as the all-encompassing, systematic mobilization of white Christian supremacist logic and morality that attacks individuals and communities by targeting a specific identity marker that is posited as evil and a dangerous threat that must be suppressed or eradicated. Markers of identity include but are not limited to race, gender, sexual orientation, language, country of origin, and religion. These conditions create a hostile environment for individuals identified with the targeted identity, because they are subjected to continuous threats of physical and psychological harm through widespread condemnation, vilification, and violation of their basic human rights.

Let's take some common challenges of the LGBTQIA+ community to illustrate the concept. Without federal legal protections, LGBTQIA+ youth have little recourse from the barrage of violence they often experience. Those in moral leadership incite bullies of every kind through their demonization of Queer and Trans people from behind podiums and pulpits. Spiritual Violence continuously follows many LGBTQIA+ youth: first with our blood families at home and condemnation at church, then with discrimination and bullying at school. All of which makes the process of growing up, figuring out who we are, and getting an education extremely difficult.

Later, we can be fired from our jobs and/or evicted from our rental homes because of our sexual orientation or gender expression, leaving us without any recourse whatsoever. Those who denigrate us—spiritually, emotionally, physically—act with impunity and even feel good about doing so, because LGBTQIA+ people have been painted as predators and a threat to children and families. Some of us find ourselves living on the streets or in abusive relationships without access to the social safety nets run by community organizations, because they are encouraged to exclude us from their services and care under the guise of religious freedom.

In daily life, we are harassed in both active and passive ways. Society constantly feeds us messages that we need to change or erase parts of our identity if we want to feel safety and belonging. Intimidation and the constant threat of bodily harm are always close when we try to access healthcare or government services like marriage certificates or a legal name change. From politicians and law enforcement to faith leaders and random bullies, there is always something trying to exterminate our community for not conforming to the status quo of gender and sexuality.

Many of us live under these kinds of life circumstances—where we can expect animosity and antagonism at every turn as part of daily life. This not only erodes our self-image and resiliency, but it also compromises our mental and physical well-being, which is borne out in many public health statistics.[27]

Thankfully this is not the whole story of our lives: love, joy, kindness, creativity, and purpose find their way through the fog of hate—for most of us. Nevertheless, these scenarios are not far-fetched or occasional outliers; they are common enough to be tropes in movies and other media, perils of life that happen over and over again in LGBTQIA+ communities. Though individually they may each seem like a personal problem, or when put together, a string of bad luck, these trials and tribulations are actually part of a larger project of Spiritual Terrorism that blames Queer and Trans people for our own marginalization and commandeers all of society—including ourselves—to collude with our annihilation.

The Ideals of white Christian Supremacy

The United States has built its cultural identity on origin myths and hero narratives that emerge from and exhaustively reinforce the values of white Christian Supremacy: the brave pilgrims, the virtuous founding fathers, the adventurous cowboys, the selfless soldiers, and the genius of those who harness the power of the "almighty dollar," etc. Through these idealized tropes, we learn a lot about social hierarchies and what we should aspire to be. A few of us check all the right identity markers, but most of us do not.

It may not be obvious at first glance how these social beliefs are connected to Christianity but understanding that white Christian Supremacy coopts all aspects of the faith to reinforce systems of power such as white supremacy, patriarchy, and capitalism, can help to connect the dots. The following are some examples of privileged identities alongside the white Christian Supremacist claims that justify their supposedly superior status:

- Being cisgender, male, heterosexual, married and head of household, because God is supposedly male and supreme ruler. According to this biblical interpretation, man (and not woman) was formed in the "image and likeness" of God to rule over his family and society as patriarch.

- Having Aryan features, because white is a symbol of purity and light. God, who is Light and good, is ubiquitously depicted with Aryan features, and God supposedly favors those who phenotypically mirror Him.

- Having wealth, because an abundance of money, land, and resources supposedly indicates divine blessing, and serves as proof of good character and righteousness.

- Being a landowner, because "God is King of Kings and Lord of Lords." He owns everything and everyone. In His stead, He has supposedly given man "dominion" over all the earth, so owning land and exploiting it to be "productive" aligns with God's intention for man and Creation.

- Being able-bodied and conventionally attractive, because illness, disability, obesity, and being unattractive are interpreted as "defects" and signs of punishment for sin.

- Being culturally Christian, because being conscripted into the ideology that legitimizes and confers these privileged statuses is mandatory.

Even though these are rarely said out loud, they are obvious in practice. The ideologies of white Christian Supremacy are so entrenched in what we know of God and what we expect from the biblical text, that we hardly need prompting to acquiesce to its biased logics. Most of us never analyze it, especially if we love God and want to be faithful. All of us have been habituated to ignore it even when it is hiding in plain sight.

What makes a person inferior, suspect, or evil has been pre-determined for us based on generations of collusion between powers—both religious and political—who have crafted and honed many corrupted versions of Christian morality to serve their own interests, and we have been taught that it is safer to just accept it as the way things are.

Becoming conscious of the ideological underpinnings and justification for Spiritual Terrorism is critically important to its identification. It is not only that at a broad institutional level Spiritual Terrorism attacks members of certain communities based on specific identities or unchangeable characteristics, but rather, that everyone, regardless of identity has been conditioned to collude with its violence.

SENTIPENSAR: IDENTITY MAP

We all embody a combination of many identities, some of which are closer to the ideals of white Christian Supremacy and therefore work to our benefit, while others are farther away from the ideal, and work against us. There are many more than the few listed in the previous section: immigration status, education, physical location, age, access to English, neurological processing, etc.

Try to create your own identity map starting with writing the ideals of white Christian Supremacy the center of a circle. Next plot your own various identities in terms of each one's proximity to the ideal. This simple exercise helps us visually understand our proximity to privilege. The higher the concentration of identity markers we carry that fall close to the center, the more privilege we have access to in a society dominated by the ideologies of white Christian Supremacy. The identity markers that fall far away from the center—literally on the margins—are marginalized identities that make us more vulnerable to Spiritual Violence which almost always exposes us to physical and systemic violence.

It's important to note that wherever our identity markers fall around the circle, whether they cluster closer to the center, on the far edges, or somewhere in between, this is not a measure of our value or worth. Rather it is a broad snapshot of where we are more at risk ourselves and where we have proximity to power that we can use to be an ally to others who are targeted by white Christian Supremacy.

We are more at risk of experiencing Spiritual Terrorism when we have more than one identity marker that is far from the embodiment that white Christian Supremacy desires. Even one marginalized identity exposes us to Spiritual Violence which can range from passive disdain to aggressive targeting. With multiple marginalized identities, such as being a Person of Color, a woman, and an undocumented immigrant for example, we are forced to confront violence on various fronts concurrently, which reduces our chances at survival.

Because those with institutional power have the most fire power and resources to wage Spiritual Terrorism, it makes it much harder for would-be victims to protect ourselves. Those who are responsible for authorizing and encouraging systemic violence conspire with each other behind closed doors to orchestrate public acts of terror. The foot soldiers of Spiritual Terrorism often attack in anonymity, either from behind masks, behind the desks of institutional bureaucracy, and/or as part of a paid and volunteer labor force who carry out the directives of those in power.

The following narrative demonstrates one pattern of how Spiritual Terrorism works in practice and helps us better understand how systemic injustice increases the vulnerability and exposure to violence for those with multiple marginalized identities.

YADIRA and EMILIO

Yadira and Emilio are a young couple from El Salvador who were too young to remember the brutality of the civil war that destroyed much of their country throughout the 1980s, but like everyone else, they live the consequences of a country thrown into political chaos, extreme poverty, and national trauma. As they fell in love and started their family in the outskirts of San Salvador, they didn't know that it was the United States of America who had sent $1 million USD per day to finance their government's bloody repression of civilian *campesinos* with more than $4 billion USD worth of weapons, military equipment and training. They didn't know that it was US military experts who trained their government's special counterinsurgency forces on how to carry out the kidnappings, torture, massacres, and assassinations that stole the lives of so many Salvadoran civilians.[28]

They grew up admiring *El Norte* as an ideal society, the epitome of success. They knew of many people who had taken refuge in the USA during the war and sent money back to support their families, who then built houses from cement rather than sticks and tin. They had friends who went to school because their uniforms and book fees were paid by remittances from relatives in the USA. From the images and movies they saw, everyone in the USA was beautiful, happy, and rich; most importantly there was no violence, no gangs, no war.

Trapped in the reality of no work to provide for their children's basic needs, Emilio and Yadira decided that he would go to the United States of America for a couple of years to work and support the family. Emilio's journey by bus, train, and then on foot was long and physically strenuous, but he made it. When his heart ached with missing home, he returned to pictures of his children, Yizel and Ilán. They were just two and four years old when he entered the desert to cross the border. But even when he felt utterly alone, he was grateful to have found work because he was proud to be able to fully support his family for the first time.

Back home, the terror of gang wars got continuously worse until there seemed to be no escape for Yadira. One day, a man on the bus who had been eyeing her for several days threatened her with a weapon, because her hair was dyed a color a little too close to the color of a rival gang. Yadira felt alone and scared. She started thinking about following Emilio to the USA to reunite their family and hopefully secure a better future for her small children. A neighbor told her how certain *coyotes*—people who work in the transport of undocumented immigrants—had a limited-time offer where children could be crossed for free with a paying adult if they were young enough to be carried. Yadira, inconsolable about leaving her homeland, but scared and desperate, quickly sold everything she could, and began her journey north with Yizel and Ilán.

After several weeks of the exhausting journey, crossing through Guatemala then into Mexico, she and others were arrested by border patrol agents at the southern border of the USA. Yadira tried to tell them that they were seeking asylum, but after arriving at a detention center, Yizel and Ilán were taken from Yadira's arms and disappeared behind a huge metal door. It was the worst moment of her life.

Days before, as part of the "Zero Tolerance" policy, the US government began to separate families that tried to cross the US-Mexico border seeking asylum. The parents were charged as criminals for having entered the USA without immigration documents. Their children, including babies still in diapers, were held in separate facilities inside warehouses full of chain-link metal boxes, herded like animals into large groups, sleeping on the cold cement floor.

Soon Yadira was shackled in a long line of chained migrant women and brought before a judge who was speaking to them in English. They were quickly processed altogether and summarily convicted for unlawful entry into the United States of America. She was transferred to another detention facility to await deportation without being able to communicate with an attorney or Emilio.

Her children, together with thousands of others from Guatemala, Mexico, El Salvador, and Honduras, were taken to a government-run shelter for children without being able to see, talk to, or know anything about their parents. Ilán cried for his mother hour after hour, day after day; the children had never spent the night away from her. Yizel held him close to her chest, rocking him and quietly repeating the prayer of protection that her parents had taught her to pray each night before bed.

For weeks on end social media buzzed with videos and images of the sad, scared, and bewildered faces of young children wrapped in thin foil sheets laying on concrete floors, locked behind metal fencing. They provoked outrage from many corners of the world. In response to this humanitarian outcry, the then Attorney General of the United States, defended the administration's immigration policies with the Bible. He said, "I would cite to you the Apostle Paul and his clear and wise command in Romans 13 to obey the laws of the government, because God has ordained them for the purpose of order."[29]

The conclusion was that there was no moral error or violation of the human rights of these children and families by the US government because the administration was ordained by God to govern as it sees fit in defense of "law and order." Therefore, any laws or decisions it makes are legitimate and blessed by God—even if those laws criminalize migrants who should legally have the right to seek asylum—and even if the separation of innocent young children from their parents causes inconceivable trauma.

Emilio searched for a lawyer to help him get his children out of the government detention center, but even with legal help, he could not claim custody of his own children because he too, is undocumented. His lawyer told him that if he presented himself to the court, he would most likely be immediately detained, charged and ultimately deported—possibly to one of the worst prisons in the world, El Salvador's mega-prison, CECOT.

With no money, no legal standing, and no political clout, Emilio and Yadira can only wait and pray as their precious young children disappear into the US system as "unaccompanied minors" with unknown futures and no legal connection to their parents who sacrificed everything to try to give them a better chance at a good life.

Within the ideologies of white Christian Supremacy, actions that would otherwise be deemed morally reprehensible become virtuous under the pretense of self-defense and community protection.

Yadira and Emilio find themselves in the crosshairs of systemic violence based on their multiple marginalized identities and circumstances, such that, even the most basic human rights become inaccessible. With nowhere to turn for protection or escape, they are at the mercy of a system of unjust laws in which they lose everything. Rather than being admired as young people who risked all they had to try to save their own lives and make a future for their children, they, like so many immigrant families, are vilified as "violent criminals" and scapegoated for their own tragedy.

SENTIPENSAR: TREE VIZUALIZATION BODY PRACTICE

The wounds of Spiritual Violence leave painful reminders in our bodies, and coming to terms with this lasting reality can be difficult. It is often accompanied by feelings like shock, hurt, anger, or helplessness. Nevertheless, we can always return to our bodies to offer opportunities for care and healing. Each time we do this, we can tap into our own restorative power to reconnect with a sense of fortitude and hope.

This visualization meditation works with the metaphor of a tree to revitalize the body by tapping into our connection to the power of the natural world.

In a quiet place or with soft music in the background, take a standing posture with your feet under your shoulders and your knees slightly bent. Try to become aware of your whole body and observe the natural rhythm of your breath throughout your body as you softly close your eyes.

Visualizing your body as if it were a tree, start by bringing your attention down to the soles of your feet. Feel each foot in contact with the floor and imagine roots growing down through the bottoms of your feet, down from your knees and legs, and from as high as your hips. The roots anchor you firmly to the ground and draw up nourishment from the earth. With each breath, go deeper into the sensation: breathe in through your roots or the bottoms of your feet, as if you were taking in nutrients from the earth. As you exhale, also towards your roots, imagine strengthening them and helping them to grow.

Now raise your attention to your legs, hips, and torso, visualizing them as the trunk of a tree. Think about how wide and strong your trunk is and use your breath to create a trunk that is reliable, flexible, and full of life. Draw energy up from the earth into your roots and carry it up to your trunk. Let that energy move into whatever does you the most good right now: flexibility, strength, rest, growth, etc.

Lastly, focus on your chest and back and feel the branches and leaves that make up the canopy of your tree. Imagine these growing from your belly button and your ribs. As you create this canopy, you decide when there are sufficient branches and leaves, and you can even choose to grow flowers or fruit as well. As before, use your breath and imagination to make your canopy leafier or greener, drawing air from your roots and carrying it wherever you want it to go.

With your transformation complete, notice if there are any scars or gashes in the branches of your tree, resulting from storms, droughts, or pests. Can you also see how nature's own wisdom has helped heal these wounds? You can also offer your tree a light drizzle of rain to be reinvigorated or a soft breeze to help free dry leaves or dislodge unwanted visitors. You can also give yourself a little shake if that feels good to you.

Finally, try to perceive the presence of other trees around you. If you are not doing this exercise in a group, you can imagine them as loved ones all around you. You can be nourished by the warm embrace of the forest, feeling shade from the bigger trees, and also feeling the protection that your tree offers to the smaller ones. You can feel the communication network that has been established among your intertwined roots. It tells you that you are not alone, and that the life force of the forest will accompany you wherever you go.

With your hands on your heart, finish this exercise with a few deep breaths to help integrate this sensation of protection and solidarity into your body. And any time you need it, you can return to your tree to fortify it as well as to find refuge and rest within.

Terror and Impunity

When marginalized people resist inequality or refuse to submit to the authority of those who oppress us, campaigns of terror frequently ensue to beat us back to our assigned place at the margins. These campaigns of terror try to keep targeted groups away from collective power through violence and threats of violence including harassment, discrimination, destruction of property, kidnapping, disappearance, physical brutality, torture, imprisonment, and even assassination.

The calculated acts of indiscriminate life-threatening harm create an unstable environment in which people are constantly on high alert. Spiritual Terrorism's intent is to intimidate, harm, destroy, cause fear, and manifest power through a show of force. The anticipation of violence and death can overwhelm victims to the point that we are so consumed by anxiety and fear that we can become despondent, apathetic, or hopeless. Spiritual Terrorism instigates fear beyond the immediate victims and infuses terror into the entire community and others who are percieved to share the targeted identity.

Perpetrators of Spiritual Terrorism are almost always free from accountability and punishment, because mainstream society and those in power are convinced that they are "doing the right thing." Some of the most familiar clichés that assuage the role enforcers play in maintaining the status quo are that they are "following the law," "defending values," "maintaining law and order," or simply "doing their job."

Those who execute Spiritual Terrorism through physical violence in the name of morality and preserving the status quo also receive cultural impunity and collusion from many in society, because order, compliance, and submission to authority—as supposedly mandated by God in the Bible—are some of white Christian Supremacy's highest values.

By flaunting their absolute impunity, those in power make an example out of those they terrorize. Impunity prohibits victims from claiming even our most fundamental rights, leaving everyone with the targeted identity vulnerable and exposed. This is meant to show others the consequences if we do not acquiesce to authority: the same terrorizing violence will befall us, either because we belong to a targeted group, or by being an ally to victimized communities.

Impunity can also be confusing and frustrating for victims and their communities who seek justice, but do not find it. This is especially true for those who do not recognize the underlying ideologies of white Christian Supremacy that motivate such violence, because our lived experience does not match our beliefs and expectations that societal systems are equitable and just.

Collective Resistance through Living Authentically

The very existence of people with marginalized identities who live ethical, positive, and successful lives debunks the moral logic of white Christian Supremacy. The basic ideological foundation for supremacy in its many forms is reasoned in the following way:

> Morality, virtue, and favor exclusively belong to those whose embodiment matches the shared societal ideal (based in white Christian Supremacy). Such

> is the natural order of things—orchestrated and authorized by God.

When we embody multiple marginalized identities, we pose an exponentially greater threat to the status quo just by living our lives out loud as our authentic selves, because each marginalized identity provides another potential avenue to refute supremacist moral claims to monopolize power. The audacity of marginalized communities to claim our personhood in its full truth and expect not only human rights, but equality and dignity, is the source of the outrage that fuels the mechanisms of white Christian Supremacy that provoke the wrath of the systemic power and its representatives through Spiritual Terrorism.

For those who do not embody the ideal phenotypes or conform to the correct behaviors as designated by white Christian Supremacy, threats and aggressions mount from all sides, manifesting in economic, psychological, social and physical ways.

Let us take the current all-out war being waged against Trans, gender-fluid, and non-binary people as another illustration:

Our very existence as gender diverse people who lead fulfilling lives, who love and are loved and accepted, who create families and contribute to the communities of which we are a part, we disprove the foundational bedrock of patriarchy. We show that gender is not a rigid, fixed male-female binary, and it cannot, in truth, be simply assigned at birth based on external genitalia, but rather it is a highly varied and fluid process of self-discovery and embodied experience.

It is no mystery then, why there is so much focus on walking back the recent cultural shifts toward inclusion and reestablishing an unquestionable gender binary for all.

To maintain their power, lawmakers, leaders of institutions, and independent actors collude in Spiritual Terrorism against gender diverse people in the name of God, hiding behind white Christian Supremacist morality. In addition to unambiguous acts violence such as bodily harm and interpersonal bullying, violence is also deployed by those in power through indirect means that shield them from direct culpability.

Spiritual Terrorism shows up through the expressed mandate of harm, such as discriminatory laws and policies; passive encouragement of harm such as demonizing or scapegoating a group of people; and/or through exemption from accountability and consequences that would normally come with inflicting violence on a person or group of people.

No Trans person can escape the calculated evil of systemic violence. However, other privileged characteristics can influence the frequency and severity of brutality. On the other hand, when gender identity intersects with other marginalized identities such as being poor, living in a rural area, being undocumented, or being a Person of Color, the danger multiplies.

Consider the ways a Trans person who is unhoused has many more forced interactions with the police than someone who owns a condo in a gayborhood, and thus, they have a higher exposure to harm. A Trans person who has not yet had access to gender affirming care or the resources to travel across state lines to get it similarly faces a higher risk of violence than their counterpart who has fully transitioned, passes as cis-gender, and has had the best medical care money can buy.

Nevertheless, across the board, Trans people have become so vilified that members of our community are constantly under attack and at risk of life-threatening violence. This experience of never being able to rest, of having no place of refuge and safety, no one to protect you from harm, and being in a state of constant alert in response to threats coming from multiple centers of power and control simultaneously, is the experience of Spiritual Terrorism.

As our lived realities as gender diverse people are more widely embraced, the legitimacy of cisheteropatriarchal power structures will continue to collapse. It has already begun, and once gender diverse people are fully accepted in mainstream society as equals, the ability to systemically auto-assign rights and privileges based on a binary gender model and to control people's bodies through mandated behavior within prescribed gender roles will cease.

Thus, we are as dangerous to the systems of domination as they claim we are, and as a result, they must try to stop us in order for those in power to maintain control.

SENTIPENSAR: DECODING THE ISOLATION STRATEGY

Isolation is a key strategy of white Christian Supremacy because it makes us feel alone and keeps us from connecting the dots of systemic oppression. Some of the most common sentiments are captured in the following statements:

- I am (or my family is) the only one who is having this problem, so it's my problem to deal with.
- Whatever is happening, it is my fault,

  because of something I did/did not do or

  because I am not smart enough to avoid the problem or

  because I am not capable enough to solve it.
- I deserve whatever is happening to me,

  because God is testing me or

  because it is God's will or

  because God is punishing me.

- It's just how the system works. I have to put my head down and get through it so I can move on.

When we are consumed with the tasks and problems of our own individual daily life and survival, we are much less likely to collaborate or organize in groups to demand change at a broader systems level. As we move toward healing, it is pivotal that we come into a greater consciousness and join the efforts of those actively in the struggle against social injustice.

Grappling with Spiritual Terrorism

The psychological warfare of Spiritual Terrorism can lead to Spiritual Trauma if the logics of white Christian Supremacy are accepted and internalized by victims. white Christian Supremacist logic masquerades as divine truth, claiming it as proof of the value, worthiness, and divine favor we seemingly lack. In other words, if marginalized people believe that God is on the side of those who wage war on our bodies and spirits, then these psychological attacks make their way inside our minds to destroy our resolve to fight back. If those who experience Spiritual Terrorism are convinced that we do not merit basic human rights and dignity, either because God has called us evil or has not yet swooped in to save us, then the systemic attacks on our self-worth make their way into our bodies to silence our soul's demand for equality and freedom. When we open ourselves up to these insidious lies and accept them as truth, we allow them to dismantle our sense of personhood on the inside. Spiritual Trauma can then ensue with profound and lasting consequences. To combat this eventuality, we must unlearn the moral scripts of domination.

One of the most valuable tools to sabotage Spiritual Terrorism is becoming vigilant to how it works and when it is at play, both individually and collectively. This is learned by understanding where we are in terms of our privileged and marginalized identity markers, as well as that of others. Whatever the situation, the ability to decipher how systems of power classify and assess the value of the people and communities involved is an asset that can support the safety of marginalized people and help privileged people use our access to power in solidarity with those who are targeted.

At the beginning of this journey, it is important to constantly remind ourselves that white Christian Supremacy is not a legitimate expression of faith, and its mandates do not originate with God or anything holy. In this way, instead of negatively judging ourselves for our marginalized identities or for not being "good enough" to meet the system's supremacist standards and expectations, we can focus on the truth that the problem does not lie with us, and no one deserves to be terrorized.

When we understand that Spiritual Terrorism in our communities is a result of systemic injustice that feeds into an entire ideological system of oppression, we can see beyond the convenient excuses of individual personal failures or divine retribution. Rather than solely attempting to individually address each act of violence as it comes, we can begin moving in solidarity with others who are also being targeted by these forms of marginalization, and our movements and strategies are fortified and increased.

Likewise, when we identify the embodied characteristics that give us privilege, we can ask ourselves how we want to use that access to power. This helps us become more cognizant of how we move through the world, and where we are acting as unwitting accomplices of those waging Spiritual Terrorism on those with less privilege.

It is also essential to develop our ability to offer ourselves grace and kindness and empathy when we feel sad, overwhelmed, distressed, or discouraged. These are normal and valid emotional responses in the face of an existence threatened by the power moves of white Christian Supremacy.

Growing our awareness of the Spiritual Terrorism suffered by other individuals and communities is not optional. It is often painful to sit with, but it is necessary to open ourselves beyond our own circumstances in order to expand our understanding. The first step is to believe marginalized communities when they tell us what is happening to them. white Christian Supremacy teaches us to distrust and blame victims rather than defaulting to a position of listening and solidarity. When we come into consciousness about what others are experiencing, and how systemic injustice is attacking them with different and similar tactics, we can affirm and accompany each other, rather than judge the struggles of others that we may not fully grasp.

Within the lived reality of white Christian Supremacy and Spiritual Terrorism, the work of critical thinking and discerning our own personal beliefs about God, goodness, and morality is an act of disobedience in a system of domination that demands our unquestioned loyalty and compliance.

Understanding our privilege can be especially challenging because it is so engrained in everyday life. In small and large ways, we have been conditioned to automatically respond to situations from a place of internalized entitlement and superiority or internalized shame and inferiority, most likely without even being present to it.

This process of decolonizing our knowledge, nuancing our beliefs, and rebuilding our moral frameworks is perilous work—emotionally, psychologically, and spiritually—which is why it is best explored and accomplished in community. It is a lifelong project that can be supported through study, critical analysis, and by being with others who are doing similar work.

To hold on to these new hard-won truths with steadfast conviction may very well lead to clashes with authority at every level of power from within our own families and communities all the way up to institutional and systemic representatives of powers. To remain faithful anyway is incredibly brave and sacred.

Even when it feels solitary, we must remember that we are not alone. It is not hyperbole to say that for as long as empire and supremacist distortions of Christianity have existed, there have been movements of people who resist it. This decolonizing work joins us to these legacies.

5: Religious Abuse

For so many Christians, church has been our safe and sacred place. The place where we could go and break open our hearts to God, where we could feel our joys and our sorrows in their rawest and most vulnerable forms. Some of us have found respite and love in a church family that helped us escape the violence of our homes. Many of us could track the journeys of our lives through the milestones celebrated at church such as Christmas and Easter times, baptisms and first communion, youth groups, life-long friendships, weddings, births and funerals.

It is precisely because these spaces are so precious to us that we must do all we can to ensure the safety of all who enter them. Those of us who cherish our places of worship bear a responsibility to root out the legacies of colonized religion that cultivate a culture of impunity—one in which Spiritual Violence is not only tolerated but perpetuated at the highest levels of leadership. While this work can be painful, it is essential for people of faith to confront the realities of Spiritual Violence and Religious Abuse within our churches in order to heal the wounds of white Christian Supremacy that defile the values of a life-giving faith.

For those who grew up in a church, we were taught reverence for our religion, its sacred texts, worship practices, and systems of belief. Many times, we were taught that respect was demonstrated through unquestioned obedience to the moral leadership of those serving in the community as ministers, teachers, worship leaders, and mentors. When that authority is abused, the harm it causes is exacerbated by the unique relationship believers have with their faith leaders.

Religious Abuse is a severe and intimate form of Spiritual Violence that specifically occurs within a church, spiritual community, or other religious-based group where a person in a position of power within the institutional hierarchy intentionally and maliciously takes advantage of a person or people who are under their spiritual care for their own personal benefit or gratification. From their ministerial role, they use their religious authority to engage in emotional, psychological, physical, sexual, spiritual, and/or economic acts that cause harm to others. Religious Abuse exploits the inherent trust and vulnerability of someone seeking spiritual care and guidance and uses it for unethical behavior that frightens, intimidates, manipulates, coerces, blames, humiliates, or injures someone who is considered a parishioner, church member, follower, believer, student, disciple, or spiritual child of that faith leader.

In Chapter 1, we focused on the body and those who have experienced Spiritual Trauma and the theologies that commandeer their agency. In this chapter we will focus on the conditions surrounding Religious Abuse that enable it to infiltrate some of our most sacred spaces. We will start again with a narrative of a lived experience and then look at the ecosystem of the church and characteristics of religious leadership in faith institutions that make believers more vulnerable to clergy who take advantage of their power. Then we will survey the theological terrain to understand the bad and good of Christian theologies that help or hinder Religious Abuse.

The treacherous contours of Religious Abuse come into focus in the following example:

JULIANA[30]

For Juliana, God was the most important thing in her life. In addition to attending services with her family on Wednesdays and Sundays, she spent several days a week at church, helping with cleaning, organizing events, or rehearsing for the choir. Singing was one of her greatest joys. She was planning to move to Argentina to study music once she finished high school in a few months, and the arrangements were all set. She was so excited!

Her family had started attending Oasis of Hope Evangelical Church when she was nine as a place of comfort and support after her parents separated. The church was led by Pastor Patricio, and the rules of the church were very strict. The pastors had to be consulted about all life decisions, including things like Juliana having a boyfriend or going to visit her father who now lived in a different part of the country.

When Juliana was 14 years old, she started dating a boy in her class at school. She had her mother's permission, but when the pastors at church found out, they were very upset with her. They told her she wasn't allowed to have a boyfriend until she was 18, and if she wanted to stay in the choir, she would have to end the relationship. Even though her mother, Elizabeth, did not approve of this controlling behavior by the church leadership, Juliana eventually relented and broke up with her boyfriend. She always wanted to choose God over her own desires, and she loved God and singing more than anything.

As time went on, Jonathan, one of Pastor Patricio's four sons, grew from being a youth leader and managing the choir to having divine revelations and visions. His influence in the church grew quickly, and soon his father named Jonathan as his successor as head pastor, bypassing standard prerequisites such as psychological evaluation or formal theological training.

Pastor Jonathan took a particular interest in Juliana and started to control who she spent time with, telling her who she should date, and even what she should do with her life and career aspirations. He manipulated her with instructions received through divine revelations he claimed to receive from God. Pastor Jonathan even created a fake Facebook profile where he posed as a psychologist and pastor named "Juan" in order to befriend 18-year-old Juliana and further control her. She received "Juan's" advice about her life, but when he didn't agree with her choices, he would cite Bible verses that scared her and threatened her with God's punishment.

The most alarming conversation between them happened when "Juan" told Juliana that God had revealed to him in a vision that she was supposed to stay home and marry Pastor Jonathan's brother, Pastor Israel, rather than moving to Argentina to pursue music.

Distraught and confused, Juliana went to Pastor Jonathan for spiritual guidance, not knowing that he and "Juan" were one in the same. He listened to her concerns and asked for a week's time to receive his own vision from God. After which, he confirmed to Juliana that God had revealed to the same vision to him, meaning that she would indeed marry his brother, Pastor Israel, who was another pastor at their church.

Juliana had a close relationship with Pastor Patricio, his sons, and their whole family. She had spent a lot of time with them at their home and at church, but she did not want to marry Pastor Israel. She wanted to go study abroad and become a singer.

Juliana's mother, Elizabeth, tried to reassure her that no one, not even the pastor, had the right to dictate her future or choose her husband. Elizabeth suspected that "Juan" was actually a fake profile created by someone in the church, but she couldn't prove anything. Becoming increasingly displeased with the church trying to control her family, especially Pastor Jonathan's smothering influence over Juliana, Elizabeth and her family left the church.

Just two months later, Pastor Jonathan kidnapped Juliana on her way to work and later murdered her, likely with the help of his brother, Pastor Israel, and their father, Pastor Patricio.

On the day she went missing, Elizabeth tried to file a police report about her daughter's disappearance. The officers in charge just reassured her that Juliana was probably just pregnant and had run off with a boy. Pastor Patricio contacted the family urging them not to involve the police. As time went on the members of the church told her to "wait for justice." To this day, many years later, Juliana's body has never been found.

Elizabeth and the rest of Juliana's community relentlessly demanded answers and tried to pursue justice on their own without success. Prosecutor after prosecutor refused to investigate the case because

Pastor Jonathan was a "devout Christian" who they presumed could never be involved in such a crime. And as Christians themselves, they refused to go against a "man of God." Ten consecutive prosecutors assigned to the case refused to examine the evidence or investigate Juliana's disappearance. Even after Pastor Jonathan admitted to creating the fake Facebook profile of "Juan" in order to provide "spiritual guidance" to Juliana, whom he believed had lost her way, no one would take the case.

Throughout the entire process, both the church leadership and members of the congregation used narratives based on "God's will" and "obedience to His anointed" to obstruct access to the truth and even went so far as to launch a smear campaign against Juliana.

Finally, after six years of constant pressure by Juliana's community, Mayra, an evangelical woman herself, was appointed as the new prosecutor. She reviewed the 130 folders of the case file, carried out exhaustive searches, and collected enough evidence to charge Pastor Jonathan. Pastor Patricio and Pastor Israel fled the country before they could be arrested, but Pastor Jonathan eventually confessed to kidnapping Juliana—though he claimed her death was an accident.

For Mayra, her Christianity wasn't a stumbling block in the pursuit of justice, rather, it was just the opposite. She credits her faith as the source of her strength and perseverance that demanded she find the truth about what happened to Juliana and do her best to see that it didn't happen to anyone else.

The Complex Ecosystem of Church

Churches have a different culture than other public spaces in society; there is a general expectation that people will be friendly to strangers and regular church members alike. With a presumption of benevolence and integrity, communities of faith are set up to be a welcoming place where people can come in times of crisis to receive emotional, psychological, spiritual, and often material support. This culture of hospitality and kindness creates different norms around things like physical proximity, touch, asking personal questions, and sharing sensitive information. All of which can be used for harm.

Things that would normally be warning signs or inappropriate behavior are socially acceptable within the trusted space of a religious community. There is an ease of physical access and emotional connection within church communities that would not be permissible in other circumstances. Communication online and in-person between faith leaders and members of the congregation of all ages is common and understood as private and confidential. Even punitive measures can be explained under the guise of moral instruction.

The Powerful Position of Clergy

Religious leaders are often deferred to as moral exemplars and spiritual guides—both within and beyond their church communities—making critiques of their leadership especially difficult. They are frequently understood to have direct access to God, which renders their decisions difficult to question, their behavior hard to admonish, and their demands nearly impossible to refuse.

In many Protestant churches, the apex position of clergy is reinforced through dynastic pastoral leadership passed from father to son to grandson, generation after generation within the same family. In Roman Catholic and Eastern Orthodox traditions, clerical authority is traced back to Jesus' apostles through apostolic succession. This situates priests as divinely sanctioned representatives of God on earth. Priests consecrate Holy Communion (understood as the real body and blood of Christ), baptize children, officiate weddings, hear confessions, confer First Communion, and administer last rites at the time of death—sacraments that, for many Catholics, are believed to determine one's eternal destiny. Clergy thus hold extraordinary power over spiritual life and death, salvation and damnation. This concentration of authority is unparalleled and makes it exceedingly difficult for believers to refuse or challenge a "man of the cloth" who exploits the reverence and trust afforded to his office.

Children and youth are especially vulnerable within these religious ecosystems.[31] In the sacred sphere of faith, sexual grooming often remains invisible or is actively misrecognized as loving care by a spiritual caregiver. Grooming manipulates theological virtues—trust, obedience, intimacy, and mentorship—transforming them into mechanisms of control. Predatory clergy may offer attention, affirmation, gifts, and special access, gradually crossing boundaries while spiritualizing the relationship.[32]

Faith leaders are not merely trusted adults; they are positioned as mediators of God's will, interpreters of sin and salvation, and gatekeepers of belonging. Practices such as confession, pastoral counseling, and spiritual direction grant clergy access to deeply intimate knowledge that can later be leveraged for coercion or imposed silence. When clergy are framed as family—reinforced through titles such as "father"—abuse becomes harder to name and nearly impossible to report.[33]

Multiple Spheres of Influence

Beyond individual actors, there exists within every faith community a complex political and social landscape that can unintentionally contribute to an environment that is rife for Religious Abuse. Because churches are nonprofit institutions that require financial resources and governing boards in order to exist, there are additional nexuses of power and influence in addition to that of the faith leader that need to be examined.

Churches are generally hierarchical spaces with a high level of authority given to a group of men in church leadership (i.e. ministers, deacons, elders, etc.).[34] Large financial contributions afford certain members of a congregation and their families more influence within the church as patrons. Likewise, governing boards, such as a board of elders or a board of directors, carry a lot of power within the community, often supervising the head pastor. Centers of influence are also created through the founding families of a church. Their descendants hold institutional memory and help maintain the culture of the community in addition to being financial benefactors.

The involvement of the pastoral family can further complicate the ecclesial ecosystem when multiple family members occupy overlapping roles within the church. The pastor typically preaches during worship services while also managing the day-to-day operations of the congregation. Pastors often provide counseling to individuals and couples, officiate family ceremonies such as weddings and funerals, and visit the sick and homebound.

In many Protestant contexts, pastors' wives serve in women's or children's ministries, mentor younger women in the congregation, and contribute to the music ministry through roles such as playing the piano or singing in the choir—often in addition to their unpaid domestic labor as wives and mothers. Older children and extended relatives of the pastor may also fill various leadership or support roles within the church. Because pastors, their spouses, and other family members are frequently undercompensated or unpaid for this labor, churches benefit financially from minimizing staffing costs while relying on the pastoral family for much needed support. At the same time, this arrangement creates a dense web of loyalty, obligation, and financial interdependence that can draw family members into complicity and make it significantly more difficult to name, challenge, or report abuses of power.

Cultures of Religious Legalism

Beyond formal positions of authority within church ecosystems, cultures of high social control function as a significant environmental factor in Religious Abuse. In many churches, belonging is contingent upon adherence to rigid behavioral codes and the avoidance of activities deemed "worldly" or morally wrong. These may include drinking alcohol, dancing, getting tattoos, dressing immodestly, gambling, listening to secular music, dating non-Christians, or engaging in sex outside of marriage.

In more conservative religious communities, prohibitions can extend further—to accessing any media not explicitly approved by leadership; using Western medicine, including emergency services, prescribed medications, or mental health care; allowing children to attend secular schools or universities; wearing makeup or jewelry; women uncovering their heads in public or during worship; or seeking help of any kind outside the community.

This system of enforcing highly specific and restrictive moral conduct—purportedly grounded in sacred texts—is commonly referred to as Religious Legalism. Within this paradigm, the Bible is treated as the literal, inerrant Word of God, and emphasis is placed on the "letter of the law" rather than the "spirit of the law." Because Scripture is subject to countless interpretations, the passages elevated for emphasis tend to reflect the culture and theology of that community. Teachings centered on self-denial, individual sin, forgiveness, discipline, obedience, and eternal divine punishment are frequently exploited in ways that facilitate abusive environments.

Within these systems, compliance with expectations of "godly behavior" is interpreted as evidence of salvation and a prerequisite for good standing. Those who follow the rules accrue social capital within the community, reinforcing cultures of control and submission to authority. Independence or dissent is framed as sinful and indicative of weak faith, deficient commitment, or moral failure. As a result, any form of nonconformity or questioning is met with severe consequences, including public reprimand, stereotyping, formal discipline, removal from leadership, or expulsion from the community.

Social cohesion in such environments is maintained through surveillance and the policing of members' behavior, often framed as mutual accountability or care—helping one another "avoid the slippery slope," "keep from sinning," or "stay on the straight and narrow." The biblical story of Cain and Abel from Genesis is frequently invoked to reinforce believers' responsibility to "be our brother's keeper." Spiritual advisors, helpers, and guides often serve as instruments of this control, relying on fear of punishment, shame, and blame to enforce compliance with communal norms.

This social structure effectively weaponizes the concepts of sin and salvation to regulate behavior and suppress dissent. Rather than centering salvation as a free gift of grace through faith, we tend to calculate our worth and goodness in comparison to others while judging others against the community's ideals of sinlessness. In this context, information becomes power, producing cultures of gossip, secrecy, of being "found out," and deep shame for any moral failures or shortcomings in the eyes of the community. Everyone strives for perfection—and inevitably fails—while jockeying for proximity to holiness and righteousness in the hope of being deemed worthy of love, belonging, and ultimately, salvation.

Such systems often give rise to stark double standards: one set of rules rigorously enforced for rank-and-file believers, and another for those in positions of power who routinely fail to practice what they preach. In these cases, abuses of authority are rarely addressed openly or transparently. Instead, they are cloaked in coded language (for example, sexual assault being described as "inappropriate behavior"), handled in secret, minimized, ignored, or left unnamed altogether.

When these hypocrisies are exposed, whistleblowers are frequently labeled as disruptive, rebellious, immature, or spiritually weak. In response, leaders who feel embarrassed or threatened may publicly attack, humiliate, or cast doubt on the reputation and credibility of those who speak out. Public chastisement becomes normalized, further consolidating institutional power while eroding the agency of believers. Over time, community members learn that love and acceptance are conditional—earned and maintained through obedience—making them more likely to remain complicit in other forms of abuse and far less likely to report harm when it occurs.[35]

Having examined the social ecosystem of faith communities, we now turn to their theological landscape to explore how conventional Christian beliefs can be co-opted and mobilized to sanction Spiritual Violence and Religious Abuse. Mariela's story introduces several of these themes and provides a point of entry for the discussion that follows:

MARIELA

Mariela is a faithful woman raised from childhood in small evangelical churches. From the time her third child, Josué, was diagnosed with cerebral palsy, she embraced her new roles in his daily medical care in addition to those she already had as mother and primary caregiver for her children. Early on, church members would approach her to say that God had blessed her with an angel, and that she should be grateful for this opportunity to serve God.

Of course, Mariela loved her little boy, but that did not alleviate how often she felt worn thin and bone tired. It seemed that every time she got one issue under control, two more popped up in its place. Every doctor's appointment and visit to the social worker felt like a struggle to get her son what he needed, and she often left feeling demoralized and insufficient. There was never enough time, resources, or support to provide the normal life she wanted for all her children.

Whenever she expressed these feelings in her faith community, though, she was criticized for her lack of faith and trust in God, who "has everything under control" and "never gives us more than we can handle." These reactions from God's saints shamed Mariela into silence, even though her body and soul felt overwhelmed every single day.

After a move to a different part of the country, Mariela's new boss invited her to a revival where a famous prophet was coming to preach. Once she arrived, she was surprised by the crowd and the atmosphere. Everyone seemed electrified with anticipation, and her excitement grew with the congregation as the praise and worship music grew to a crescendo. Finally, the Prophet made a dramatic entrance and was welcomed with applause and euphoria. Mariela listened with rapt attention, but it wasn't just his words that struck her. He was calling people to the stage and healing them!

"God wants us to be well...to be whole, healthy, and flourishing!" was the first thing that caught her attention. "Sickness doesn't come from God, but from the Devil!" He shook his fists in the air, fighting the unseen forces of evil.

Mariela's heart trembled, and she wondered about what she had believed her whole life. She had always thought that God blesses sacrifice and rewards all those who suffer with humility. *What if this holy man was right? Could her faith take away some of the suffering in their lives?*

"If you want to see God's healing hand in your life, you have to demonstrate that you are committed to Him," continued the Prophet. The choir began to sing again and people carrying large baskets began to walk among the congregation.

"God wishes you to bless this place with your gifts so that He may bless you in return."

More people deposited their money into the baskets as they walked or were carried to the stage. In each case, the Prophet laid hands on their body and prayed over them. He cited their offerings as proof of their faith, and he prayed to God to heal them and bless them in equal measure with their faith. He called out the demons causing their illnesses, and with each healing he would scream, "Arise and go forth: your faith has made you whole!" Mariela remembered those words from the Bible. Many people cried and shook with emotion, some shouted giving praise and testimony to their healing.

Mariela watched in awe. In her heart, she prayed, *"Ever since I was a child, I have been obedient to you, God. I would do anything for my little Josué to be healed."* Just at that moment, the Prophet yelled, "How much are you willing to give God to show Him you are ready to receive a miracle?"

I would give my life, Mariela responded with all her heart and soul.

Back home that night, while Mariela fed Josué, her mind was full of doubts and questions. *If disability comes from Satan, what did I do that my child would be punished so?*

*...The doctors say that there is no cure, but the Prophet says my baby can be healed with enough faith...*Mariela felt uneasy. *How can I show God that I am ready for a miracle if we can barely get by?*

She debated whether to take Josué to the Prophet the next night and offer her meager life savings for his healing. It wasn't much, but it was all they had. *Would it be enough for a miracle?* she wondered.

As she drifted off to sleep, other Bible phrases came to her prayerful mind, *For nothing is impossible for God...Your faith has made you whole...Go and sin no more...Blessed are the poor in spirit, for theirs is the kingdom of heaven.*

SENTIPENSAR: INTERPRETING THE INTERPRETER

The Bible is a powerful force in our world. Its words can be used to comfort, heal, accuse, and condemn depending on who is wielding it and why. Pay careful attention to the ways that the Bible is used in your contexts. Remember that it is possible to interpret each verse in a myriad of ways; there is no singular correct interpretation of the Bible.

As a rule, biblical interpretations say more about the intentions of the person explaining the text than they do about the text itself! It is always a good idea to keep the context and worldview of the speaker in mind as you receive their take on a text. Be aware that when the Bible is being used to punish, condemn, or control, it is possible that the text is being manipulated for other purposes.

Theologies Leading to Exploitation

It is often difficult for those outside of the faith community to understand how Religious Abuse happens, particularly among adults. Economic exploitation is a prime example of how Scripture and faith get weaponized for greed.

For instance, it is not uncommon for people to volunteer their time or talents to their faith community. However, certain volunteer roles that the community depends on, such as church musicians, are often expected to work an inhumane number of hours each week to demonstrate their commitment to God and maintain good standing within the community. Anything less than what is expected, for any reason, is seen as a moral failing and a disappointment to God. People are regularly dismissed from their leadership positions and judged harshly by the church when they need to decrease their weekly time commitment and responsibility. This is a form of economic Religious Abuse that often gets overlooked because it is so common.

In some ministries, like the one in Mariela's story, religious leaders use their spiritual authority in order to extract financial resources from believers through tithes and offerings. Their teachings promote the ideology that wealth is synonymous to possessing God's favor and blessing. Known collectively as prosperity gospel, seed-faith gospel, or the gospel of success, they preach that the more wealth we obtain, the closer we are to God.

Consequently, receiving God's blessing (i.e. wealth) is directly connected to the strength of one's faith. In these contexts, faith is expressed primarily through giving money to the church or other Christian ministry, which in turn goes to the institutional leadership who use it for their own personal benefit. Unsurprisingly, their flagrant show of wealth becomes the proof of their faith and status as God's chosen spiritual leaders, which feeds into the ongoing cycle of economic abuse.

For those who struggle financially, they are especially encouraged to give, with common phrases like "Give until it hurts!" The narrative of the widow's mite in Mark 12 is often invoked as the exemplar, since Jesus praised the widow for giving from her poverty. Though it was not a lot of money, it was significant to Jesus because she gave "everything she had, all she had to live on."[36] That feeling of desperation is something many elderly, poor, and working-class people can resonate with. In this ideology, giving money to the ministry is a way of planting a financial seed which God will supposedly bless and send back to the giver multiplied hundredfold.

The Bible does not narrate the outcome of the poor widow's life after giving the Temple her last coin. Jesus certainly did not promise her financial security, but this Scripture is effectively leveraged as a sign of faith and trust in God for those who also give out of their poverty. Prosperity ministries exploit money from millions of people worldwide—many of whom are in dire financial crisis and most in need of receiving economic support rather than giving it to opulent clergy who abuse the Gospel.

Theologies of Bodily Harm

In addition to Religious Abuse promoted through the theologies of money, the role of toxic Christian theologies of the body cannot be overstated. In this section, we will take a look at some of the theological beliefs that create the conditions for abuse in quick succession.

Within the ideological frameworks of the faith, illness and disability can undermine the personhood of those who live with them, because these are often framed as a consequence of sin and/or demonic forces. Even in the narrative above, the focus is on Mariela rather than Josué. We never learn of his thoughts or feelings. Sometimes the bias is explicit, as it is in prophet's healing ministry. Other times, it is implied through a focus on Jesus' healing miracles and ideological frameworks where salvation and faith equate to health and ability.

Believers who struggle with mental health, trauma, neuro-divergence, obesity, infertility, chronic illness, and/or a disability often feel unwelcome in faith spaces. Sometimes our "afflictions" are invisible or go completely ignored, and so we feel unseen and misunderstood. We suffer in silence and isolation. Other times, we are seen as a project for Christian charity, or we become a case study in the healing power of prayer, exorcism, and other religious healing rites. The most common experiences include feeling judged for our trials and tribulations and blamed for our failures of faith when we are not miraculously healed.

Similarly, "conversion therapy" and "reparative therapy" are erroneous terms intended to reinforce the idea that LGBTQIA+ people are somehow ill, confused, possessed by evil, or mentally unwell. Framed in faith spaces as an internal moral battle between good and evil, "struggling with same sex attraction" conjures disdain, judgement, and/or pity. These abusive pseudoscientific practices almost always originate in faith-based organizations and often involve talk therapy, aversion therapy (e.g. electric shock), chemical or surgical castration, brain surgery, "corrective" rape, prayer and laying on of hands, physical isolation, assault and exorcisms.[37]

Despite the extraordinary diversity in every part of Creation, the scientifically-proven biology, the parallel behaviors of thousands of animal species, and the countless Indigenous cultures and ancient societies that prove the contrary, many Christians continue to believe that God—Creator of the vast and expansive universe—made only two genders (male and female) and one sexual orientation (heterosexual).[38] For these Christians—including LGBTQIA+ Christians—any deviation from heterosexuality and cisgender is, at best, an illness to be treated and cured, and at worst, an abomination punishable by death and eternal damnation.

Christian doctrines about gender that emerge from the ideologies of white Christian Supremacy are deeply embedded in our collective psyche. Within Christian societies more broadly, we are socialized to accept particular power dynamics and gender-based theological violences as normal—or even as righteous and divinely ordained. Let us take a closer look:

Traditional biblical interpretations have taught us that woman originated from the rib of man, and that we were created to be helpers rather than leaders and protagonists. Consequently, many women's sense of worth comes from our labor as caregivers and our roles as wives and mothers. In families, communities, and churches, women carry a disproportionate responsibility for the unpaid physical and emotional labor, and financial resources needed to maintain them.

In the narrative we don't find out if Mariela is married, which is unusual in and of itself. A woman's status as married or single is most often one of the first things we learn about someone. What we do know is that she is the primary caregiver of her children, and she works as well. The glorification and romanticization of a woman who can "do it all" is connected to the theological ideas of biblical womanhood that are lauded in Proverbs 31. Here, she works and provides for her family financially while also taking care of her assigned domestic responsibilities alongside being the primary caregiver to her entire household.

When Mariela feels overwhelmed and exhausted, the response from her community of faith is one of judgement rather than support. Her struggles are a personal failure, rather than a systemic problem. She is expected to be a radiant Proverbs 31 woman.

No one sympathizes with her plight, perhaps because they also have similar burdens, or perhaps it is because many Christian traditions link suffering and sacrifice with holiness and salvation. We are also taught that it is divinely ordained that women should endure the pain of childbirth and sacrifice our own bodies through our lifelong labor for the care and comfort of our families, communities, and churches. In cases of Religious Abuse, this theology of prioritizing those around us and freely giving ourselves to others at the expense of our bodies can easily extend to submit to our spiritual leaders to give them whatever they desire from us.

A variety of biblical texts are used to endorse a gender ideology that claims that women's bodies are not our own. Ownership first belongs to God, then to our fathers, and eventually to our husbands. Should we birth children, we will necessarily share our bodies with our babies for a time.

Many women's groups at church teach that the primary purposes of marriage are to have children and to keep our husbands from lust. Pre-marriage, we are told to deny our own urges for sexual pleasure to save our bodies for our future husbands, and then afterwards, wives are taught that we should never deny our husbands sex because our body belongs to him.

Because we are made to believe that the body is suspect and a conduit of sin, we ignore its warning signs and try to defy its physical and emotional limits. Practices of disciplining the body in order to rid ourselves of vices (like pornography or overeating) or to focus on God are also widely encouraged within Christianity. Devotional practices (like fasting or mortification of the flesh) are widely accepted as evidence of holy devotion, and many Christians throughout history have withheld their own bodies' basic needs—sleep, food, water, sex, companionship, shelter, etc.—to commune with God.

Christian notions of martyrdom glorify sacrifice even beyond the physical sense; giving one's life for the faith is highly honored. It may sound like hyperbole, but these communally held ideals shape the thoughts and expectations of believers. They define what we are willing to submit to versus what we resist. The phrase, "to suffer as Christ suffered" or "to suffer with Christ" taken from 1 Peter 4 is used to encourage believers to accept suffering as something we must endure to grow in our faith.

Broadly, the disdain and deprioritization of the body make concerns about vulnerable bodies less important. The primary focus for most churches is a spiritual one: to save people's eternal souls and thereby store up treasures in Heaven rather than being overly preoccupied with concerns of the flesh on this earthly plane.

SENTIPENSAR: SUPPORTING CHANGE BODY PRACTICE

Our joints are the physical mechanisms we use to move our bodies; they can represent our willingness to change course or to be flexible to adapt and progress. Through simple exercises like this one, we can support our bodies in connecting with the internal forces of resilience that make it easier to begin a new day, a new routine, a new job, or to even take a new step in our healing process.

From a standing position, relax your legs and bend your knees slightly. Move your feet parallel to each other, shoulder width apart. Looking forward, drop your shoulders and let your arms fall to your sides. For better relaxation, do a quick, vigorous shake, releasing the most recent tensions from your body. Next, tune into as many of your joints as you can, from your feet up to your head, moving them gently as you move up the body and become aware of them. For example, you may perceive your toes or your knee; wiggle them to acknowledge each one tenderly.

This can be developed into a routine of rotating and stretching each one of your joints seven times, each in linear movements first (backwards and forwards or side to side) and then circular movements. This will help cold joints warm up safely, since linear movements require less strength than the circular ones.

Let's begin with your toes. You might use the floor to add pressure when pushing your toes back and forth. Continuing with your feet, go up and down on the balls of your feet, stimulating your ankle, seven times before beginning to rotate your ankle seven times to the left and then seven times to the right on each foot.

Then, rotate your knees by lifting and lowering each leg back and forth before rotating it in both directions. Next, with knees bent, make circles with each of your hips, first in one direction, then the other.

Since each vertebra is a joint, we can bring movement to the joints in our spine by gently twisting and moving. Become conscious of each vertebra and try to move it in different directions to reach each part of your spine.

Next, focus on the joints in your arms—shoulders, elbows, wrists, and fingers—first making linear movements and then rotating them in both directions.

When we get to the neck, we can similarly move our head, first backwards and forwards, and then to each side. For circular movement, it's best not to go in a full circle. Instead make a crescent moon shape motion in a forward direction by placing your chin on your chest and then raising your head up to the right and then up to the left, trying to touch your ear to your shoulder on each side. Rotating your head backwards is not recommended for all people, so we will not do it in this exercise.

Finish up by closing your eyes for a moment and perceiving any new sensations in your body after this exercise. This routine can be done regularly to start your day or before beginning any activity that requires concentration and energy.

white Christian Supremacy would have us believe that we should discipline our bodies and ignore its basic needs and desires. It tells us that such punishment will elevate us and make us closer to God. However, dualistic ideologies that claim that the body and soul are separate or that the body is just an earthly vessel for the soul do not originate in Christianity or even ancient Judaism. In fact, the premise of the body as lowly and prone to sin because it has material needs while the soul is the encapsulation of the higher self that can ascend to God by denying the body actually comes from ancient Greek philosophy that was imported into Christian doctrine by early scholars who were part of the elite class and subject to the authority and approval of the Roman Empire. For as long as these death-dealing ideologies have connected Christianity to empire, there have been faithful scholars and believers refuting and resisting them.

Present-day Christian liberation theologies hold diverse holistic views of the body as an integrated whole together with the soul and psyche rather than a conglomeration of incongruent parts. Trauma demands that we pay attention to our embodiment, and Spiritual Trauma requires us to stitch our compartmentalized selves back together if we are to heal. Liberation Theologies redeem the body as a source of revelation and liberation. They remind us of the enfleshed nature of the Divine and bring the suffering of marginalized bodies to the forefront as a primary concern.

Liberation theologies center lived experience, particularly the experiences of those who suffer unnecessarily under the weight of systemic injustice and oppression. Latin American, Black,

Queer, Trans, Womanist, Mujerista, Feminist, and Disability liberation theologies (among others) emerge from and attend to the lived realities of specific communities that have been historically marginalized and oppressed. These traditions rebuke the fracturing of body from spirit and resist the separation of the material world from an abstract, detached spiritual realm, insisting instead that theology is made in and through lived struggle.

Liberation theologies insist that faith without action is insufficient. Their teachings call Christians not only to interpret the world but to participate in its transformation by addressing the concrete, material conditions that produce suffering. This includes practices of care such as mutual aid, accompaniment, advocacy, and community-based healing, as well as collective resistance to structures that perpetuate harm. Justice and liberation are not optional add-ons to belief but constitutive practices of faith itself.

These theological frameworks explicitly challenge white Christian Supremacy's fixation on individualism, moral perfection, and personal sin. Instead, they emphasize collective responsibility, relational accountability, self-respect, and communal repair. Suffering is understood not as an individual failure to be corrected, but as a social and structural reality that demands communal response and sustained action. Liberation is therefore measured not by internal belief alone, but by transformed relationships, redistributed power, and the restoration of dignity to those who have been harmed.

By affirming the interdependence of all Creation, liberation theologies compel Christians to confront the bodies being sacrificed on the altars of systems of domination—capitalism, white Supremacy, imperialism, and others—including our own body. Transformation and healing begin in the spheres of influence where we hold the most power: our daily, embodied practices. Choosing how we use our time, money, privilege and how we engage in relationships becomes theological work. Small, intentional actions—setting boundaries, practicing consent, interrupting harm, cultivating rest, and building networks of mutual support—become acts of resistance that sustain long-term transformation.

An aid for identifying our experiences with Religious Abuse can be found in the Reflective Awareness Tool in Appendix 3, and practical entry points for healing are offered in Appendix 4.

Closing Thoughts

Replacing theologies of harm with more liberating ones can support survivors and allies in recovering a spiritual connection to the body and restoring faith after experiences of Spiritual Violence, Spiritual Terrorism, Religious Abuse, and Spiritual Trauma.

When we are able to name experiences that previously went unnamed, we begin to make sense of our lived realities and initiate our own processes of liberation. For this reason, learning the conceptual frameworks of religious phenomena that defile the Christian faith—as presented in this book—and demystifying how they operate is itself a revolutionary act of self-claiming.

This text has saught to identify and analyze the ideologies of white Christian Supremacy as they solidify into theologies of harm masquerading as religion. These beliefs are then mobilized into dehumanizing practices that sustain systems of domination and justify a continuum of violence—from hurtful words and judgmental attitudes to genocide and global ecological destruction. Through this work, and through other educational tools grounded in lived experience, embodied wisdom, and rigorous intellectual inquiry, we aim to offer liberative healing strategies that incite action for justice on behalf of those who are being harmed.

Because trauma impacts the body, brain, and spirit, each requires attentive care for healing to take place. There is no white savior who will swoop in and rescue us from this precious, painstaking work. The labor pains of transformation and rebirth instead call us to co-create another world—and a more just, life-giving faith.

Spiritual Violence:
A Visual Representation of the Weaponization of Religious Phenomena

We end this book with a visual analogy of white Christian Supremacy and how it transforms religion into various armaments that serve systems of domination. Here we can imagine white Christian Supremacy as a weapons factory. The ideologies of white Christian Supremacy take raw materials and put them together and manipulate them to manufacture a variety of weapons that inflict differing levels of harm, from mild bruises all the way up to fatal wounds and mass destruction.

In this case, the raw materials that white Christian Supremacy draws from are things like the Bible, Church doctrines, and Christian religious traditions. Instead of supporting believers along a sacred spiritual path, they are stolen from faith and bastardized to legitimize and prop up patriarchal culture, legacies of greed, white supremacy, and imperialism. The dual forces of power and religion create the arsenal for inflicting Spiritual Violence that wreaks havoc at all levels of society. Neither would be as strong without the complicity of the other. For example, the Bible alone is not inherently harmful; it can and has been used to liberate souls and bodies for millennia. However, when it is decontextualized and put at the service of patriarchy or white supremacy, the Bible becomes a weapon of mass destruction, creating a false morality that sanctions generations of violence and domination.

Factory as white Christian Supremacy

This weapons factory, like white Christian Supremacy, does not look evil at first glance. Its imposing Neoclassical architecture reminds us of important and official buildings all over the western world: the US Capitol and the White House in Washington DC, Buckingham Palace in London, the Arc de Triomphe in Paris, El Capitolio in Havana, and the original: the Pantheon in Rome. Its grand scale, prominent columns, simple geometric forms, and stone facade all evoke the military power and political domination of the ancient Roman Empire. All buildings made in this style are employing the same strategy; they are claiming the legacy of an all-powerful, conquering empire that colonized millions of acres of land and dominated a fifth of the world's population. These buildings are meant to elicit feelings of solemnity, respect, and deference by appealing to our modern-day cultural admiration of an empire's patriarchal ideals of masculinity, dominance, order, and control.

The ideologies of white Christian Supremacy use the images and language of Christianity just as Neoclassical architecture draws on the cultural heritage of the Roman Empire. Many of us comply with its logic at first glance without probing deeper into whether we truly agree with its presuppositions on right and wrong. We are culturally preconditioned to respond to things that sound like Christian morality with deference and respect. Just as white Christian Supremacy is actually systems of domination parading around in the stolen robes of Christianity, the imposing structure of the weapons factory make it look commanding and legitimate. Opaque glass windows give the perception of transparency, but hide the nefarious enterprises going on within. Sometimes the ideologies of white Christian Supremacy are hard to identify among the costumery of religion, just like the only signs of the large-scale weapons production in the drawing are the plumes of air pollutants coming from the smokestacks and tiny details on the building's insignia.

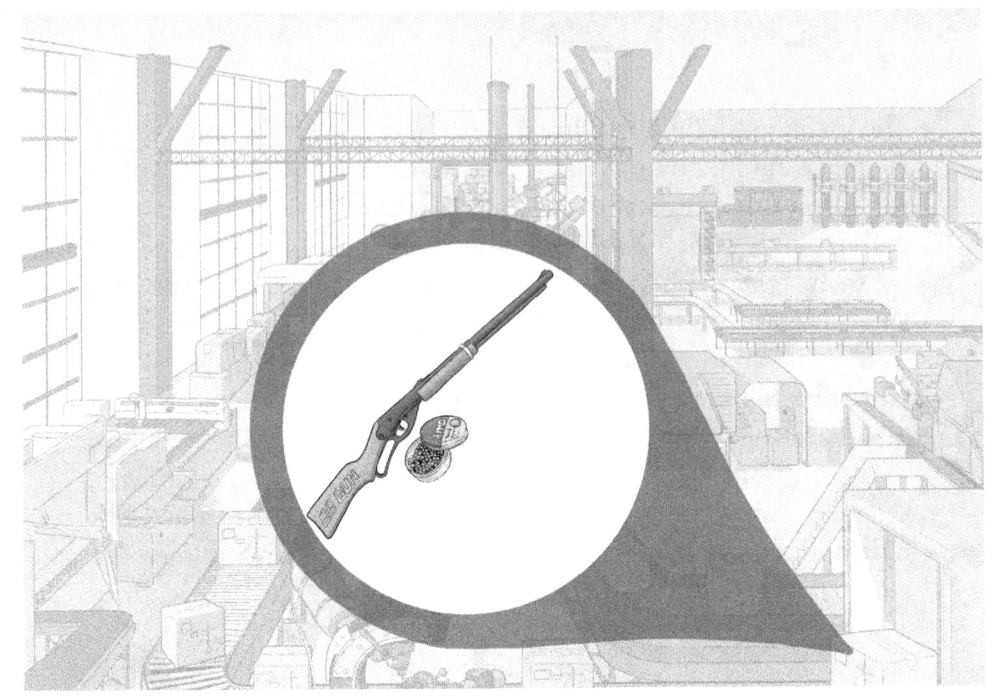

BB Gun as Daily Spiritual Violence

In this analogy, the weapons being produced range from a spring-action BB gun to a nuclear bomb. Each has its own intended purpose and target. Of the weapons in this analogy, low-powered BB guns are the simplest design, the most common and easiest to access. They use metal projectiles and generally cause non-lethal damage to targets at a fairly close range. Each time a shot is taken, the weapon must be reloaded or recocked before it can be aimed and fired again. Though significant injuries can occur, fatal wounds are seldom the intention or the outcome. Similarly, the most common Spiritual Violence that the majority of us encounter in our daily lives is made up of small insults and unkind actions that are meant to hurt our feelings or humiliate us. These often induce emotions like anxiety, sadness, shame, fear, and anger. This level of violence does not usually kill us in one shot, rather the damage accumulates over time with numerous and repeated experiences of harm.

Handgun as Religious Abuse

The handgun best represents the concept of Religious Abuse in that the deadly harm it inflicts usually occurs in an intimate space at close range with premeditated malicious intent. The nature of the relationship between a perpetrator and a victim of Religious Abuse is necessarily one of unequal power in which one person is considered a spiritual authority with institutional backing while the other is considered an individual follower who is not only supposed to be open, honest, and vulnerable with their spiritual guide, but is also expected to submit to their leadership. This kind of violence usually happens on a one-on-one basis in a close personal relationship that is supposed to be based in trust within the sacred space of a religious institution or faith community. Like a handgun shot at close proximity, the consequences of Religious Abuse are severe, life-altering, and often interlaced with other forms of violence such as coercion, exploitation, and sexual abuse.

Machine Gun as Spiritual Terrorism

Spiritual Terrorism is shown here in the form of a machine gun. It is instantly recognizable for those of us in the United States as the weapon of choice for many mass shootings. Its visual presence alone evokes fear, representing danger for an entire community of people rather than just one individual. It is a fully automatic, military-style weapon that is meant to quickly obliterate many victims in rapid-fire succession. The ammunition is bigger and more lethal than bullets from a handgun or BBs, just as the institutional power behind Spiritual Terrorism makes it deadly to entire communities who share a targeted identity marker.

Most children in the United States practice active shooter lockdown drills in their schools. While these practices were created for safety and preparation should a shooting occur, it can also stimulate a perception that one is constantly in danger, and at any moment violence could kill everyone in the community.

This sense of constant fear and alert, even in places that are supposed to be safe, represents the intention of Spiritual Terrorism. Like a machine gun, the intention of Spiritual Terrorism is not to threaten a single individual, but rather to terrorize an entire group of people with the constant looming threat of persistent and extreme violence against not just one person, but many people within the community. Sometimes the violence happens indiscriminately and at long-range, but it always carries the intention of causing extreme fear beyond its immediate victims.

Explosives Vest as Internalized Spiritual Violence

Internalized Spiritual Violence is the harm we replicate against ourselves as a result of being subjected to the ideologies of white Christian Supremacy. Once we begin accepting its harmful lies as truth, we enforce its control and punishments onto our own minds, spirits, and bodies—up to and including death. In this visual representation of a vest covered in explosives, the individual is technically in control of their own violent demise. Nevertheless, what drives them to such an extreme act of desperation and self-harm is strongly influenced by the beliefs they have internalized about the world and their own value and self-worth. One's lived experiences constantly reinforce feelings of superiority or inferiority. Without an understanding of systems of power and oppression within the morality of white Christian Supremacy, it is easy to internalize what we experience as truth and become our own worst enemy and enforcer. Additionally, just as the devastating and deadly impacts of an explosive belt reach far beyond the person wearing it, a suicide always reverberates throughout an entire community, causing pain and suffering far beyond the point of detonation.

Conclusion

A critical dimension of this analogy between white Christian Supremacy and a weapons factory is the centrality of human agency. As is often noted in debates on gun control, weapons cannot fire themselves. Violence is the consequence of human actions. The production of physical armaments, like the production of ideological ones, is the result of people who conceptualize, create, and deploy them for destructive ends.

When violent ideologies and human action converge on a mass scale, they generate the most extreme forms of religion-based violence. Within the weapons factory analogy, the nuclear bomb represents the apex of destructive capacity. Similarly, conquest, genocide, and colonization constitute the most devastating expressions of weaponized Christianity. Fueled by ideologies of hate, moral superiority, and fear mongering, nuclear weapons are meant to exterminate all forms of life and utterly obliterate any resistance to its domination. Likewise, white Christian Supremacy has historically functioned as a legitimizing moral framework for the widespread dispossession and attempted erasure of entire peoples, cultures, spiritualities, and ways of life.

At the same time, the analogy underscores that Spiritual Violence operates along a continuum. From quotidian microaggressions to intimate abuse, communal terror, internalized harm, and mass atrocity, these forms of violence differ in scale and intensity, but share a common ideological origin. They emerge from the same systems that extract religious symbols, texts, and moral authority from their spiritual contexts and reconfigure them into instruments of social control. The existence of religion alone does not produce Spiritual Violence; rather it is the subjugation of faith to supremacist ideologies that weaponizes it for harm.

This reality further foregrounds our collective ethical responsibility. It is always human beings that are responsible for building the bomb or pulling the trigger, whether in the physical sense of armed violence or in the ideological sense of weaponized religion. Both can inflict serious wounds that extinguish life, therefore both require significant human discernment and accountability.

Human agency is implicated not only in the perpetuation of Spiritual Violence, but also in its disruption. The identification of white Christian Supremacy as an ideological system—rather than a theological inevitability—opens space for taking responsibility, activating resistance, and the possibility of dismantling the structures the produce Spiritual Trauma.

The prophetic imagination of Scripture offers such a reorientation. Isaiah 2:4 envisions a future in which instruments of death and destruction are transformed into life-sustaining tools:

> They shall beat their swords into plowshares and their spears into pruning hooks; nation shall not lift up sword against nation; neither shall they learn war anymore. (NRSV)

This vision reminds us of the Christian hope of a world shaped by humility, mutuality, and the refusal of domination—a theological horizon in direct opposition to the logics of white Christian Supremacy.

Just as weapons can be disarmed and factories can be shut down, the ideologies of white Christian Supremacy can be challenged, deconstructed, and replaced with spiritual practices and beliefs that prioritize justice, equity, and the flourishing of all life.

By acknowledging our collective complicity and committing ourselves to transformative action, we can disrupt the cycle of harm and reclaim the liberatory potential of faith.

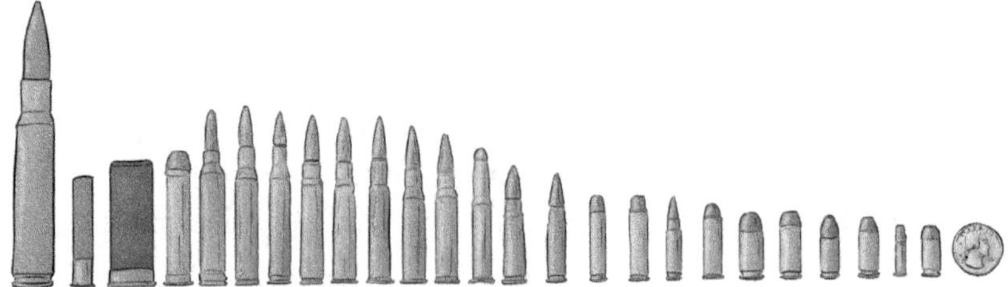

Appendix 1: Spiritual Violence Reflective Awareness Tool

The following list of "I" statements can help you assess if you may have experienced Spiritual Violence. Many people who answer "true" to any of the statements below identify as survivors of Spiritual Violence, even if the experience happened at an earlier time in their lives.

True or false...

1. I have been a part of a religious family or community of faith that regularly categorizes people as good or bad, worthy or unworthy, and then accepts them or rejects them based on that classification.

2. I have been taught to distrust the messages from my body and my mind related to my own emotions, needs, and desires, because I was made to believe that my body is inherently deceptive, carnal and driven to sin.

3. I have felt guilty for not going to church because I worry that I am abandoning God. And/or I have been scared to leave a community of faith even after they caused me harm, because I felt like I needed to go to church in order to be a good Christian and have covering.

4. I have deferred to the decisions made by the men in my family even when I strongly disagreed, because I was taught that men are the rightful head of the household and have the ultimate authority to control the money and discipline the family, even when that includes corporal punishment like hitting, spanking, etc.

5. Regarding gender identity and sexual orientation or sexual practices, I have been told that "God loves the sinner but hates the sin," which sometimes makes me feel unlovable.

6. I have been profiled or experienced violence from law enforcement or other authority figures because they perceive my identity (race, gender, work, immigration status, etc.) to be suspicious and prone to wrong-doing.

7. I have accepted physical, psychological, or emotional violence or have stayed in an unhealthy relationship dynamic, because I believed that I did not deserve better.

8. As a child, I was taught to be quiet and submissive because of religious ideas like honoring your father and mother and obeying your elders. This may have continued even in situations of abuse or physical/emotional harm.

9. I have not lived out the fullness of my sexuality as a single person or a Queer person, because I was led to believe that having sex outside the institution of marriage is fornication and morally wrong.

10. I have carried guilt and shame for not living up to the religious ideals and expectations of my family.

11. Phrases like "the will of God is," or "the Bible says," have been used against me or others like me to control my behavior, condemn me, or justify bad things that have happened to me or others like me.

12. I have experienced unwanted catcalls, sexual advances, insults, threats of violence, or been sexually assaulted, and I was made to believe that I was at least partially at fault because of the way I was dressed, my mannerisms, or my behavior in public.

13. I have hidden or lied about some part of my identity, because I feared how I would be treated if others found out the truth.

14. I was made to feel that my body is less desirable and unworthy of care because it does not meet mainstream beauty standards.

15. Someone in authority over me tried to control my clothes, my behavior, and/or my language while telling me that it was out of concern for my safety and their fear that I would be judged, discriminated against, or assaulted.

16. I was taught that suffering is good because Jesus suffered for me and suffering brings me closer to God.

17. I have pre-emptively left my church or the Christian faith entirely, because I feared condemnation, punishment, rejection, or exclusion for who I am or what I have done.

18. I have been led to believe that being LGBTQIA+ is a test and my cross to bear. Even though I know I am loved by God, I have been taught that acting on my sexual orientation is an abomination, so I have considered or practiced celibacy as

an alternative way to live so I could please God, my family, and/or my faith community.

19. Since childhood I have been subjected to comments, value judgments, and jokes that made me feel like I am less capable or valuable than others because of my gender, disability, neurodivergence, age, etc.

20. I have abstained from masturbation or tried not to let my body get aroused sexually out of fear that it is morally wrong or dangerous, and/or I have been told that the Bible says masturbation is a sin.

21. As a young person, I was labeled as misguided, rebellious, or a disappointment for having my own dreams or being true to myself against my family or faith community's wishes.

22. I have been led to believe that LGBTQIA+ people should not get married or have/adopt children, because God designed families to be made up of one man and one woman for the purposes biological reproduction which is required for biblical marriage.

23. I have been called indecent (or worse) by someone in a position of religious or moral leadership and/or I have been the target of gossip because of my sexuality or perceived sex life.

24. I have been told that I am going to Hell and/or I have been made to feel like God was punishing me because of who I am or something I did.

25. I have been shamed, made fun of, or felt embarrassed to disclose my marital or familial status such as being divorced or never married, having children out of wedlock, having a blended family, or never having children, etc.

26. I have gone to pastoral counseling or "conversion therapy" or "reparative therapy" or participated in religious rituals to pray for a change in my sexual orientation or gender identity.

27. I have received derogatory comments or disparaging jokes or I have been made to feel less than others because of my race, language, culture, or religion.

28. I have been made to believe that I was born with original sin and therefore I am unworthy of grace and abundant life and must be saved because I owe an unpayable debt to God.

29. I have experienced systemic discrimination and not having the same access to basic necessities like health care and civil rights because of moralistic interpretations of the Bible and Christian theology. For example, when a government denies abortion care to those who need it, refuses marriage licenses to same-sex couples, or denies Trans people hormone therapy by arguing that the Bible or individual religious beliefs forbid it.

30. I have been made to feel broken or unfavored by God because I physically can't or don't want to have children.

31. I have been criticized by Christian faith leaders or other religious people for participating in marches, protests, civil disobedience, or other activism for human rights that "disturb the peace" and challenge the status quo.

32. I have felt that it is my obligation to give my partner access to my body even when I was not in the mood for sex or affection because I was taught that the Bible says my body does not belong to me, but rather to my spouse or partner.

33. I have been taught that my addiction is a sin rather than an illness.

34. I have stayed in a marriage even after I was certain I didn't want to be there because I was afraid I would disappoint God or fail my family due to the vows I had made before God and/or my church to stay together until death.

35. I have felt exposed and vulnerable when Christians told me that they would pray for me, because it felt as if they were calling in a higher authority to either change me, punish me, or "heal" me.

36. The religious beliefs I was taught about sexuality and pleasure have kept me from exploring things like same-sex attraction, alternative relationship structures such as polyamory, and/or non-conventional sexual practices like kink and using sex toys.

37. I have been made to feel that my disability or illness is directly connected to a lack of faith or a punishment for sin.

38. As a single person, I have been led to believe that I am not complete until I find "my other half" and get married.

39. I have been shamed for having sex with or living with someone who I was not married to.

40. After losing someone I love, people tried to comfort me with religious tropes that made God responsible for my loved one's death such as, "Heaven needed another angel." Or "This is all part of God's perfect timing, and we just have to trust His plan."

This instrument is a Reflective Awareness Tool designed to support healing, self-understanding, and validation of lived experience. It is not a clinical or diagnostic tool. While it may evolve into a validated psychometric measure, it is currently offered for reflection and community empowerment. Developed in collaboration with theologians, psychologists, and healing-centered researchers.

This text was originally published in *Violencia Espiritual y Fenómenos Religiosos Que Abusan de la Fe.* Vargas, Karina, Alba Onofrio, and Judith Bautista Fajardo. Soulforce, 2022. ISBN 978-1-7361267-6-9.

Appendix 2: Cultivating Healing Practices after Spiritual Violence

Here we offer some ideas for how to begin the journey of recovering our wellbeing after experiencing Spiritual Violence to learn about our own most whole and authentic selves in the fullness of life.

Studying History: Re/learning about our past allows us to better comprehend how Christianity has been used for evil. Investigating how religion has been complicit in systems of domination along with its motives and control mechanisms helps us identify how it shows up in our daily lives on a personal, cultural, and/or political level.

Telling our Stories: A frequent maneuver of white Christian Supremacy is to silence dissent and repress collective discord in order to protect its power and abusive leaders. Isolation can kill us. Telling our stories and hearing those of others is a powerful form of dispelling shame and guilt, consequently healing and connecting us to others. When we are brave enough to break the silence around the violence we have endured, we often find that we are not the only ones who have had these experiences and carry these wounds.

Growing in Community: When we stop putting ourselves in spaces that promote white Christian Supremacy or in the company of people who inflict Spiritual Violence through judging, denigrating, or excluding others based on their Christian morality, our bodies and spirits get a chance to come down from a state of being constantly vigilant. By surrounding ourselves with people who affirm our agency, bodily autonomy, and human dignity, our most authentic selves can feel safe enough to come out, and our best selves can be truly accepted, encouraged, and celebrated.

Responding to Violence: While we can greatly reduce our exposure to religion-based violence by making different life choices, everyday occurrences of Spiritual Violence are inevitable. Everything from living in a hostile environment to visiting family to passively consuming social media can all lead to experiences of Spiritual Violence.

In order to heal, it is important to create strategies for how we will respond when these experiences happen so that the spiritual harm does not get internalized and cause even more damage. There is no perfect strategy to accomplish this, but our goal is to apply our self-knowing and creativity to grow lives where we can safely be who we are and where we can live our spirituality freely and deeply despite living in a culture of white Christian Supremacy. Working together, we can create spaces for inclusion, freedom, and dignity for all of us.

Practicing Disobedience: The mandate of compulsory obedience and submission to authority has been misused and abused at every level of society and justified by the idea that God commands it. Often, they are equated with love and respect or even patriotism. This prevailing belief, along with the fear of punishment if we do not comply, leads us to suppress our capacity to discern many things for ourselves. When we dare to question authority or resist passive obedience to things we don't agree with, we may risk a negative consequence, but we also grow our agency, the power of deciding what is right and wrong for ourselves. Even tiny acts of disobedience, like going in the "out" door or walking on the grass, help us break the tendency of mindlessly going along with the status quo. By taking responsibility for every decision we make, even the seemingly inconsequential ones, we re/build new habits based in self-determination.

Doing Theology: A primary tactic for maintaining white Christian Supremacy in its place of power is to control information and demonize inquiry, labelling curiosity as a lack of faith. Limiting community access to independent theological education, critical biblical analysis, and outside tools for spiritual reflection maintains the status quo by denying believers the chance to question, doubt, study and reflect theologically. Exploring different ways of thinking and believing, such as liberation-based or Queer theologies, helps us mature in our faith. By stepping out of our comfort zones to try on new ideas and beliefs, we can rebuild connections to the Divine through intentional spiritual practices that resist the unquestioning obedience and submission to authority that many of us were taught growing up.

Exploring Other Forms of Spirituality: white Christian Supremacy falsely proclaims itself as the only true and faithful way to cultivate our spirits, but nothing could be further from reality. Human experience throughout the world offers a great diversity of spiritual paths, and we have the option to learn about them and their communities, discover ourselves within their beliefs and frameworks, and respectfully walk alongside them if we so choose. As we meet other people with different spiritual practices, our awareness of our own path and what works for us naturally expands. Nevertheless, as we explore, it is still imperative that we remain attentive to the patterns of Spiritual Violence, because they can appear in any spiritual path or faith tradition.

Changing our Language: One sure-fire way to begin to change our white Christian Supremacist programming and heal the wounds of Spiritual Violence, is to replace the violent messages of judgement or hate with words of kindness, love and self-compassion. This is both in relation to others and to ourselves. Instead of repeating messages like "I'm not (or you're not or we're not) good enough" or "God couldn't possibly love me (or you or us) like this," fortify yourself and others with messages like "God loves me/you/us just as we are" or "I/you/we are beautifully and wonderfully made! Amen!"

Observing the Violence We Replicate: Remaining alert to the messages that reproduce Spiritual Violence in ourselves and in our communities helps us interrupt the cycles of harm that we can often unknowingly participate in. Being able to identify and name Spiritual Violence raises our awareness so that we do not replicate them.

Some questions to ask are: What are the logics of white Christian Supremacy that I replicate without being self-conscious of them? When do I use Christian morality to criticize or police others' self-expression? In what ways do I censor and punish myself, consciously or unconsciously, at home, at work, at church or school, which deteriorates my life and my relationships? Do I ever feel morally superior to others or apathetic to suffering? When something bad happens, do I automatically assign the cause to God's testing or punishment? Where do these thoughts and behaviors come from?

Engaging in Activism: Finding ways to be an active part of the change we want to see in the world not only helps us build community with like-minded people, it can also restore a sense of purpose and connection to something bigger than ourselves. There are countless worthy causes to support, and it is never too late to join movements for social justice and solidarity in caring for life and dignity for all of Creation.

Focusing on Self-care and Joy: Using alone time to reflect on our journey rather than avoiding or shutting down and then prioritizing quality time to cultivate our inner life and re/build our self-worth supports the recovery of the strength and dignity necessary to create new ways of being in the world. Simple daily practices like taking deep breaths, resting, dancing, and returning to your own rhythm and sense of timing can be invaluable in the process of healing. Taking time to intentionally pursue joy, even amid grief, reminds us to grow into the fullness of life's emotions and experiences. It is important to remember that leaning into self-love, compassion, joy and self-care are revolutionary acts of resistance and resilience.

Seeking Professional Help: Spiritual Violence can impact us in many ways and can have long-lasting consequences for our lives. Many of these wounds and traumas are not identifiable at first glance and are best addressed working with people who are professionally trained to accompany us. When it is possible to access mental health support, dedicating the time and space to process our experiences and prioritize our healing journey can be decisive in our success.

This text was originally published in *Violencia Espiritual y Fenómenos Religiosos Que Abusan de la Fe.* Vargas, Karina, Alba Onofrio, and Judith Bautista Fajardo. Soulforce, 2022. ISBN 978-1-7361267-6-9.

Appendix 3: Religious Abuse Reflective Awareness Tool

The following list of "I" statements can help you assess if you may have experienced Religious Abuse. Those who answer "true" to any of these statements may identify as survivors of Religious Abuse regardless of when or how many times these events occurred.

True or false...

1. I was sexually assaulted or abused by a church leader or someone in a ministerial role in my community of faith.
2. I have experienced unwanted sexual advances, flirtations, and/or physical touch by someone in a position of power or protected by someone in a position of power within my faith community.
3. When serving a ministry of the church, I have been expected or pressured to work long hours and give a lot of my time and talent for little or no pay as an offering to God. And I

didn't feel like I could object, reduce my time commitment, or decline and still be in good standing with the pastor and the church.

4. I have felt afraid to question a leader in my community of faith because of their position within the church or because of their relationship to God.

5. I have been disciplined, reprimanded, or excluded for questioning or disobeying a particular teaching of a faith community or its leader.

6. My relationship with God is frequently associated with feelings of fear, shame and guilt.

7. I have felt I needed the approval of my pastor or priest in order to feel good about my spiritual life.

8. I have experienced the contradictions between what the leadership of my faith community teaches versus what they do, but I didn't feel like I could speak up about it.

9. I have had the experience of living a double life, so that I could appear one way at church and with religious people close to me while living differently in the rest of my life.

10. I have been pressured to attend counseling sessions with a faith leader to try to change my sexual orientation or gender identity.

11. Because of my gender, sexual orientation, relationship status or physical condition, I have been denied the opportunity to live into my ministerial vocation or other positions of leadership within my faith community.

12. I have felt that my trust was betrayed or violated by a faith leader, teacher, or spiritual counselor when they disclosed or

misused personal information about me or my family that was shared in confidence.

13. I was taught that I cannot enjoy the fullness of God's blessing without the covering of a religious leader or the guidance of a faith community.

14. I have been singled out as a "favorite" among my peers by someone in a ministerial role and received individual attention, gifts, outings, or mentorship that later felt dubious, coercive, or abusive. Or I have been judged in my faith community after rejecting the favoritism or advances of someone with authority in the community.

15. I have encountered hostility, judgment, and/or condemnation in my faith community for disagreeing with statements like, "Wives obey your husbands", "God made Adam and Eve, not Adam and Steve", "God said, 'Be fruitful and multiply,' thus children are the fruit of a successful marriage," etc.

16. I have been given the image of God as a severe, hard to please, male king-judge who is constantly watching us and judging our thoughts and actions, ready to punish us if we do anything wrong.

17. I have been led to believe that my faith wasn't strong enough because of the judgments of a religious leader or their followers.

18. I felt like my opinions and feelings were not considered in my religious community, even for things that impacted me. Instead, the opinions and feelings of the leader in charge of the group or community were centered as most important.

19. I felt like I couldn't tell anyone about an experience of

inappropriate behavior I had with a minister or religious leader because of their relationship with my family or because I thought I wouldn't be believed.

20. Threats of judgement, punishments, and Hell are frequent topics in the sermons and teachings of my faith community.

21. I have felt like I couldn't express my questions and doubts when I haven't understood Bible passages or teachings, because they were given by a person with religious authority.

22. I have prioritized obedience and submission as the supreme commandments, even when it troubled my conscience.

23. I have felt uncomfortable with the level of physical affection or invasive questions by a leader in my faith community, but I haven't felt supported and safe enough to say anything about it.

24. I have been taught to believe that it's normal for a religious leader to publicly degrade those who do not submit to the rules of the faith community, labeling them as "sinful," "outside of God's will," "lost," "worldly," etc.

25. I was forced to submit to payers or have experienced physical or sexual assault during a "healing" service that was supposed to exorcise my demons or cure an affliction.

This instrument is a Reflective Awareness Tool designed to support healing, self-understanding, and validation of lived experience. It is not a clinical or diagnostic tool. While it may evolve into a validated psychometric measure, it is currently offered for reflection and community empowerment. Developed in collaboration with theologians, psychologists, and healing-centered researchers.

This text was originally published in *Violencia Espiritual y Fenómenos Religiosos Que Abusan de la Fe.* Vargas, Karina, Alba Onofrio, and Judith Bautista Fajardo. Soulforce, 2022. ISBN 978-1-7361267-6-9.

Appendix 4: Cultivating Healing Practices after Religious Abuse

Below, we offer some ideas for where to start the healing process after experiencing Religious Abuse. We start with our own narratives and then place them in a larger contextual framework to open up possibilities for connection, healing, and wellbeing.

Intentionally Disobey the Rules: Because obeying the rules, compliance, and submitting to authority are so central to Religious Abuse, practicing small acts of disobedience can be helpful in reorienting our awareness to pay closer attention to when we are capitulating to authority out of habit, and when we are intentionally consenting to following the rules for safety or shared values. Try tiny rebellions like eating dessert at the beginning of your meal, going around an empty post and rope stanchion maze rather than zig-zagging back and forth through it, or telling the TSA officer at airport security that you don't want to be photographed, and explore how it feels in your body so you can strengthen the muscle of noncompliance.

Feel, Acknowledge, and Embrace: Healing inevitably involves feeling, acknowledging, and embracing our emotions. In the power dynamics of Religious Abuse the victim's desires, thoughts, and emotions are constantly being trampled, manipulated, or ignored. Naturally this leads to difficulty expressing thoughts and emotions, both in the time of experiencing abuse and in the future. All this unreleased energy generates trauma and difficulty experiencing emotions. This is why a healing process must give these emotions and thoughts the opportunity to come out and be received with dignity by a therapist or community that recognizes and validates them. Sharing may be painful, but it is also helpful and enormously liberating.

Create Healing Environments: Healing requires the companionship and support of others. Just as the community plays a key role in our spiritual lives and formation, it is similarly essential in healing processes. We can experience healing in many settings and in many ways: whether it's in support groups, conversations with family, friends and other survivors, or meditation and art spaces. The journey of personal healing is easier if we can find others who are also moving forward. The path together moves us all closer to collective healing.

Share Our Stories: It's amazing what can be healed by sharing our story with others. We experienced it in the spaces of dialogue and support that prompted the birth of this book. Sharing our painful memories and experiences in a safe and trustworthy space not only helps us become more aware of the implications and consequences of our experiences, but it also encourages others to come forward, to express their pain and share their stories, because they can see that they are not alone. And, at the same time, it helps us develop empathy to better understand each other and have patience with one another as we learn about the diverse forms and opportunities for healing that life and a liberating spirituality can offer us.

Advocate for Structural Change: Alongside these actions for personal healing, it is also important to scope out and find ways to support broader healing and bring about a more just society. Talking about religion or spirituality has its complexities, which is why many governing bodies have abdicated their role when it comes to matters involving religion. The justice system, for example, has largely left issues of Religious Abuse in the hands of those in charge of religious spaces. However, when the harm comes from the inside, it is a bit like leaving the fox in charge of the henhouse.

Almost all governmental institutions, companies, and communal spaces have rules and protocols to identify and intervene in workplace discrimination, abuses of power, gender-based and domestic violence, sexual harassment, etc. Religious spaces are social institutions within our societies, and they should not be exempt from accountability. It is possible to take into account the particularities of faith in religious spaces and simultaneously name relationships of abuse and to prevent harm and seek transparency, accountability, and restitution when abuse occurs.

Engage in Intersectional Dialogues: Interdisciplinary dialogue brings an abundance of perspectives to the work of addressing abuse by looking at broader categories and approaches to the social dynamics, political history, and impacts of religious discourses and ideologies. Different sectors of society—social scientists, theologians, activists, legislators, etc.—have come together in the past to articulate different forms of violence and potential strategies for addressing it, such as domestic violence, gender-based hate crimes, and sexual harassment in the workplace. Similar intersectional, interdisciplinary conversations about Religious Abuse and Spiritual Violence are urgently needed.

Find Professional Help: Religious Abuse is one of the most severe forms of Spiritual Violence. It can easily become Spiritual Trauma and have devastating consequences for our lives. These wounds and traumas are often complex and multifaceted and are best addressed while working with people who are professionally trained to accompany us on our healing journey. When it is possible to access mental health support, dedicating the time and resources to process our experiences and prioritize our healing is well worth the investment.

Have Faith in the Process: Healing takes time. That's not a popular truth in a world of quick fixes that constantly pressures us to speed up. It may seem easier to just put the pain away and deny the situations that caused it, but this only delays healing and exacerbates the wounds. In the aftermath of Spiritual Violence and Religious Abuse, it is important to remain steadfast in the mantra: "You heal while you live, you live while you heal." This allows us to move forward in healing, celebrating our progress made, whether big or small, as well as lovingly welcoming the areas where we are still learning and growing.

This text was originally published in *Violencia Espiritual y Fenómenos Religiosos Que Abusan de la Fe.* Vargas, Karina, Alba Onofrio, and Judith Bautista Fajardo. Soulforce, 2022. ISBN 978-1-7361267-6-9.

The Community of Lxs Sinvergüenzas

From our earliest memories our families have made it abundantly clear that they don't want us to be *sinvergüenzas*, a label reserved for "nasty" women and social outcasts. The expectations of a good woman are clearly laid out before us; she is one who is morally upstanding, obeys the rules, and controls herself at all times—principally her mouth and her sexuality. From birth we are reprimanded with, "A girl should be seen and not heard!" Becoming a good *Christian* woman means adding to that the element of submission; she is one who never contradicts her father, her teachers, her bosses, her husband, or her priest or pastor. We are surrounded by "good" women who spend their entire lives trying to achieve this perfect ideal, and so often, it costs them their lives.

It is from this white heteropatriarchal Christian supremacist context that we, the community of *Lxs Sinvergüenzas*, emerge as living examples of resistance. Our aspiration is to activate, inspire, and fortify each other and those who are like us. We are transcontinental Queer feminists from Latinx contexts who are not ashamed of our faith or our politics and activism. They grow together. We weave community to find each other across borders, across silos, across movements, across denominations and across identities. We co-create sacred spaces where we come to know each other and our authentic selves, where we are safe to strip away the layers of shame and armor covering our hearts and protecting our souls. We are sexual dissidents of all flavors, gender outlaws, fallen women and holy troublemakers. You will find us in the pews and on the streets, in the academy and in our family homes. You will find us everywhere, because we have always been here, and we always will be.

Although our very existence is a threat, we challenge the foundations of cisheteropatriarchy just by being ourselves. *Lxs Sinvergüenzas* is a digital platform and activist community conceived from many conversations with Queers, feminists and human rights defenders across the hemisphere who had been fooled into believing that faith and feminism could not even co-exist, much less mutually inform and nourish each other.

In March of 2020 during the COVID-19 pandemic lockdown, we launched the Teología Sin Vergüenza (TSV) videocast, which was the first of its kind in the region. Each episode featured a live conversation in Spanish between three academically trained Latinx theologians from across Latin America and its diaspora in the US who employ Queer-Trans feminist theologies in their everyday life and work in the academy, in communities of faith, and/or in their faith activism. The two co-hosts were Rev. Dr. Lis Valle-Ruiz and Rev. Alba Onofrio—one an academic and artist, the other an activist, both ordained pastors. Each conversation seeks to answer the core questions of this media project: How can we bridge the knowledge of the academy, the faith of the church, and know-how of Queer-Trans feminist activists across the Americas? And together, how can we transform the religious conditions that are denying equal rights and freedom to our communities and killing our spirits?

Years later, TSV continues to provide inclusive religious leadership through accessible educational resources, spiritually-healing content, and supportive community for Queer-Trans feminist Latinx activists & allied people of faith, now with English podcast episodes on the Shameless Theology podcast channel. *Lxs Sinvergüenzas* are faithful co-conspirators of new realities: we gather to share resources and strategies that strengthen our work all over the region.

As *Sinvergüenzas*, we confront the fear of being boxed in and dismissed for holding our faith and politics together. Many of us have been called naïve and disloyal to our liberation movements because we cling to our faith while at the same time being questioned and excluded from religious spaces because of our LGBTQIA+ identities and feminist commitments. We navigate the liminality of *ni de aquí, ni de allá* across many places and spaces.

We are not ashamed of who we are or what we believe, and we refuse to dissect ourselves into compartmentalized pieces to appease other people's discomfort. Together we can propose new theologies, open and inclusive communities of faith, liberating spiritualities and movement strategies—all of them free from shame and provoking others to lift their hands and voices and recover their divinity—without shame.

To stay connected and learn more about the Community of Lxs Sinvergüenzas, find us on our website (soulforce.org) or follow us on social media at @teosinverguenza. As we say on the internet, *"Somos Lxs Sinvergüenzas, ¿Eres tú unx de nosotrxs?"* (We are Lxs Sinvergüenzas, are you one of us?)

About the Authors

Reverend Alba Onofrio is a public theologian and spiritual activist rooted in the US South engaged in human rights work for over 20 years primary in the US and Latin America. As a Queer Feminist Evangelical pastor, their ministry works at the intersections of religion, gender and sexuality to heal the wounds of spiritual violence and weaponized religion. They hold a Masters of Divinity from Vanderbilt Divinity School and serve as a Global Presbyter for The Fellowship of Affirming Ministries (TFAM).

Also known as Reverend Sex and co-founder of the Sexual Liberation Collective, their global education work aims to eradicate shame and fear around bodies and sex in order to reclaim pleasure and desire as potent centers of sacred knowledge, healing, and spiritual praxis.

Through their current position as Executive Director and Spiritual Strategist for Soulforce, an international LGBTQ+ social justice organization, Reverend Alba Onofrio has published a series of theological resources on liberatory approaches to the Bible and uncovering the ideologies of white Christian Supremacy that have been translated into seven languages and distributed worldwide. They are the founder and host of Teología Sin Vergüenza, a primarily Spanish language, digital platform and podcast focused on Queer-Trans Latinx feminist theologies with an online following in over 47 countries.

Judith Bautista Fajardo is a Colombian educator, artist, and priest of the RCWP Roman Catholic Women Priests. Interfaith theologian and Queer activist, founder of the spiritual community *En Todos Tus Nombres*. Judith holds a PhD in Education with a specialization in Pedagogical Mediation and Biopedagogy; she is a specialist in the Development of Affective Processes with an emphasis on Aesthetics and Embodiment. She has postgraduate studies in Transpersonal and Integrative Psychotherapy and Anthroposophical Psychotherapy from Goetheanum Dornach, Switzerland.

As a composer, writer, and editor, her publications include *Memoria colectiva, corporalidad y autocuidado: Rutas para una pedagogía decolonial, Danzando la resurrección de los cuerpos, Destellos de Tormenta Azul y Como Espada de Dos Filos*, a finalist for the 21st Fernando Rielo World Prize for Mystical Poetry. She is co-author of the magazine: *Shemá 2: Perspectivas de Inclusión en el Evangelio de Juan y la Antología Palabras para el Encuentro*, and the musical works: *Mesa de Fraternidad, Minga de la Esperanzam*, and *Desacostúmbrame*.

She currently teaches at the Universidad Pedagógica Nacional in Columbia, and is a consultant in the areas of art, body, human development, and spirituality. She is a leader in developing art and body pedagogies for peace with communities affected by violence. Through her platform, *JBF Sendas de Vida*, she promotes La Ñapa, a weekly program of theological and spiritual reflections on current events, and her YouTube channel, which is followed by Spanish speakers in nearly 15 countries.

Nadia Arellano Tapia is a survivor of Spiritual Violence and an intercultural facilitator from Mexico City. Her work lives at the intersection of human rights, queer and feminist theologies, and resistance to religious fundamentalism. She has accompanied families of victims of violence, feminist women of faith, and religious communities committed to LGBTIQA+ liberation, supporting collective organizing, political education, and spiritual healing. She serves as the Director of Narrative and Storytelling and Director of Latin American Programming at Soulforce and is part of multiple networks, collectives, and seminar spaces working across faith, gender, and justice, where she focuses on dismantling white Christian supremacy and nurturing liberatory spiritual practices rooted in curiosity, solidarity, and community.

Notes, References, and Suggested Reading

Prologue

1 *Abya Yala* is an indigenous term from *el Pueblo Kuna* of Panama and Colombia. It is the name of respect and identity given to the "Americas" and particularly used in decolonization work and Indigenous activism.

2 *Ni de aquí, ni de allá* is a phrase that expresses a common sentiment of those born or raised in the US, but whose families come from a different country. It tries to get at the feeling of never fully belonging to the place our families come from nor the place where we grew up: "neither from here, nor from there." It conveys the lived experience of a liminal identity, in which we somehow are from both places and yet from neither at the same time. For me, this shows up in the question: "Where are you from?" asked to me almost every day of life growing up as a Brown child in white Appalachia. The question is straight-forward, but the answer is not a simple one. My theoretical

approach to this concept is deeply informed by the work of the Queer Chicana feminist and philosopher, Gloria Anzaldúa.

See: Gloria Anzaldúa, *Borderlands/La Frontera: The New Mestiza.* 2nd ed. (San Francisco, CA: Aunt Lute Books, 1999), ISBN 9781879960572.

Introduction

3 In my experience, international feminisms in the Global South are very different than US feminisms. While each context has their own specificities and internal debates, and none are without bias and prejudices, I have found these subaltern feminist movements across multiple continents to be the "big tent" that provides a gathering place for sexual and gender minorities. It's also worth noting that in many Global South feminist spaces, I have met many heterosexual, cisgender sex workers who identify as sexual minorities and organize alongside LGBTQIA+ activists in the struggle for human rights and dignity. When I refer to feminists in this book, these are the communities I am referring to. I have been incredibly humbled and honored to be invited into these sacred spaces over the years.

4 Because "white" as a racial category has always been a fictitious, ever-moving target decided by those with the power to enforce it, I do not capitalize it as a proper noun under any circumstances (even at the beginning of a sentence).

Chapter 1: Spiritual Trauma

5 American Psychological Association, "APA Dictionary of Psychology: Trauma," accessed January 1, 2025, https://dictionary.apa.org/trauma.

I use the APA definition of trauma as a starting point for

talking about Spiritual Trauma, because I do this work as theologian and pastor rather than a mental health professional. My intention is to nuance the conversation on trauma from a Queer, feminist theological perspective.

6 This true first-person narrative was written by Nadia Arellano. The author's real name is used here by her brave and vulnerable request.

7 For more on this topic, see the following suggested publications:

Judith L. Herman, *Trauma and Recovery: The Aftermath of Violence—From Domestic Abuse to Political Terror* (New York: Basic Books, 1992), ISBN 9780465061716.

Kathy L. Kain and Stephen J. Terrell, *Nurturing Resilience: Helping Clients Move Forward from Developmental Trauma—An Integrative Somatic Approach* (Berkeley, CA: North Atlantic Books, 2018), ISBN 9781623172035.

Renee Linklater, *Decolonizing Trauma Work: Indigenous Stories and Strategies* (Halifax: Fernwood Publishing, 2014), ISBN 9781552666623.

Pat Ogden, Kekuni Minton, and Clare Pain, *Trauma and the Body: A Sensorimotor Approach to Psychotherapy* (New York: W. W. Norton & Company, 2006), ISBN 9780393704570.

8 Written by Nadia Arellano.

9 For more on this topic, see the following suggested publications:

Bessel van der Kolk, *The Body Keeps the Score: Brain, Mind, and Body in the Healing of Trauma* (New York: Viking,

2014), ISBN 9780670785933.

Resmaa Menakem, *My Grandmother's Hands: Racialized Trauma and the Pathway to Mending Our Hearts and Bodies* (Las Vegas, NV: Central Recovery Press, 2017), ISBN 9781942094470.

Chapter 2: white Christian Supremacy

10 For more on this topic, see the following suggested publications:

Ramsay MacMullen, *Christianizing the Roman Empire (A.D. 100–400)* (New Haven, CT: Yale University Press, 1984), ISBN 9780300036428.

Peter Brown, *The Rise of Western Christendom: Triumph and Diversity, A.D. 200–1000*, 10th Anniversary rev. ed. (Malden, MA: Wiley-Blackwell, 2013), ISBN 9781118301272.

11 For more on this topic, see the following suggested publications:

Bartolomé de las Casas, *A Brief Account of the Destruction of the Indies* (1542; Project Gutenberg, 2007), https://www.gutenberg.org

Chris Mato Nunpa, *The Great Evil: Christianity, the Bible, and the Native American Genocide* (Tucson, AZ: See Sharp Press, 2020), ISBN 9781937276645.

Robinson A. Milwood, *European Christianity and the Atlantic Slave Trade: A Black Hermeneutical Study* (Bloomington, IN: AuthorHouse, 2007), ISBN 9781425950477.

Katharine Gerbner, *Christian Slavery: Conversion and Race in the Protestant Atlantic World* (Philadelphia: University of Pennsylvania Press, 2018), ISBN 9780812250237.

Adam D. J. Brett and Betty Hill, "Documenting Domination: From the Doctrine of Christian Discovery to Dominion Theology," Religions 15, no. 12 (December 2024): 1493, https://doi.org/10.3390/rel15121493

12 Nicholas V. "Dum Diversas (Papal Bull), June 18, 1452," in *European Treaties Bearing on the History of the United States and Its Dependencies to 1648*, ed. Frances Gardiner Davenport (Washington, DC: Carnegie Institution of Washington, 1917), 20–25.

13 Alexander VI. "Inter Caetera (May 4, 1493)," in *European Treaties Bearing on the History of the United States and Its Dependencies to 1648*, ed. Frances Gardiner Davenport (Washington, DC: Carnegie Institution of Washington, 1917), 71–78.

14 For more on this topic, I suggest looking into the many resources of Doctrine of Discovery Project: https://doctrineofdiscovery.org/

15 For an accessible entry point into this topic see: Alba Onofrio, *What You Need to Know About the Bible* (Soulforce Spirit Resource Library, 2017), ISBN 978-1-7361266-4-6.

16 I understand that several colonizing countries were also colonized such as Portugal, Spain, Italy, the United States, etc., thus making these exact terms impractical. However, the original intention of showing the biased and supremacist nature of language and terms like "underdeveloped nation" remains.

Chapter 3: Spiritual Violence

17 See Genesis 1:26 and for an accessible entry point into this topic see: Alba Onofrio, *Breaking Open: Genesis 1—The Gender of God & Creation* (Soulforce Spirit Resource Library, 2017), ISBN 978-1-7361267-0-7.

18 See the story of Deborah in Judges 4.

19 For an accessible entry point into this topic see: Alba Onofrio, *Breaking Open: Gender Diversity in the Bible* (Soulforce Spirit Resource Library, 2022), ISBN 978-1-7361267-5-2.

20 Claiming the historical Jesus of Nazareth to be Trans, is a wonderful theological conversation starter on gender because it quickly reveals our socialization around gender, gender bias, and lack of theological imagination. Many Christians are immediately defensive about this claim, which begs the question, *What upsets us about the idea of Jesus not being a cisgender, heterosexual man?*

Biologically speaking, some use an argument that because Mary, the mother of Jesus, conceived Jesus through the Holy Spirit rather than a human father, then Jesus did not receive a Y chromosome (since Mary would have only possessed X chromosomes). Consequently, Jesus would have genetically had only X chromosomes, which would have made him biologically female. By this logic, he could be considered Trans if he lived his life as male but had the chromosomes of a female. Another genetics argument suggests Jesus could have been Intersex similar to someone with De la Chapelle syndrome where a person who is assigned male has XX chromosomes.

Theologically speaking, Jesus could be understood as Trans for a number of reasons. First God is *Trans*cendent, meaning that God's gender is more expansive than human categories of sex and gender. Some Christians would say that God doesn't have a gender and therefore is agender or genderless. Conversely, because God is referred to in the plural form (see Genesis 1:26), and because God is the 3-in-1 (i.e. the Trinity), and because Jesus is considered fully human and fully divine, some would say that God's preferred pronouns could be "they" and "them" similar to many genderfluid, genderqueer, and nonbinary folks. Next, Jesus is Trans because he undergoes multiple *Trans*itions and *Trans*formations from eternal God into mortal human flesh (with a name change to Jesus) and then back to eternal God through the resurrection. Finally, in John 19:34, when a Roman soldier pierced Jesus' side with a spear when he was on the cross, water and blood emerged from his body. For many, this is birth imagery, but coming from a man, thus representing Jesus as a person of *Trans* experience.

Regardless of the different arguments, I am most convinced that Jesus suffers with those who suffer through the companionship of the Holy Spirit. In the same way that James H. Cone connects the body of Jesus on the cross to Black bodies on the Lynching Tree and other "crucified people of the world." I believe Trans bodies are sacred, made in the image and likeness of the Divine, and when they are crucified, Jesus is again crucified through them.

For more on this topic, see the following suggested publications:

> Alex Clare-Young, *Trans Formations: Grounding Theology in Trans and Non-Binary Lives* (London: SCM Press, 2024), ISBN 9780334065532.
>
> Christina Beardsley and Michelle O'Brien, eds., *This Is My Body: Hearing the Theology of Transgender Christians*

(London: Darton, Longman & Todd, 2016), ISBN 9780232532067.

James H. Cone, *The Cross and the Lynching Tree* (Maryknoll, NY: Orbis Books, 2011), ISBN 9781608330010.

21 Onofrio, Alba. *Breaking Open: Genesis 1—The Gender of God & Creation.* (Soulforce Spirit Resource Library, 2017), ISBN 978-1-7361267-0-7.

22 Ibid.

23 For an accessible entry point into this topic see: Onofrio, Alba. *What You Need to Know About the Bible* (Soulforce Spirit Resource Library, 2017), ISBN 978-1-7361266-4-6.

24 *1946: The Mistranslation That Shifted Culture,* directed by Sharon "Rocky" Roggio (2022), documentary film.

25 For an accessible entry point into this Scripture see: Alba Onofrio, *Breaking Open: Sodom and Gomorrah*, ed. Yaz Mendez Nuñez (Soulforce Spirit Resource Library, 2016), ISBN 978-1-7361266-5-3.

26 For more on this topic, see the following suggested publications:

Bruce Bagemihl, *Biological Exuberance: Animal Homosexuality and Natural Diversity* (New York: St. Martin's Press, 1999), ISBN 9780312253776.

Joan Roughgarden, *Evolution's Rainbow: Diversity, Gender, and Sexuality in Nature and People* (Berkeley: University of California Press, 2004), ISBN 9780520240735.

Chapter 4: Spiritual Terrorism

27 Recommended websites to access LGBTQIA+ health statistics:

Williams Institute, "Identity, Stress, and Health of LGBTQ People in the US," UCLA School of Law, accessed January 1, 2025, https://williamsinstitute.law.ucla.edu/visualization/lgbt-toplines/

Centers for Disease Control and Prevention, "Health Disparities Among LGBTQ Youth," accessed January 1, 2025, https://www.cdc.gov/healthy-youth/lgbtq-youth/health-disparities-among-lgbtq-youth.html

U.S. Department of Health and Human Services, Office of Disease Prevention and Health Promotion, "LGBT," Healthy People 2030, accessed January 1, 2025, https://odphp.health.gov/healthypeople/objectives-and-data/browse-objectives/lgbt

28 For more on the United States intervention in El Salvador, see:

Lesley Gill, *The School of the Americas: Military Training and Political Violence in the Americas* (Durham, NC: Duke University Press, 2004), ISBN 9780822333920.

William Blum, *Killing Hope: U.S. Military and CIA Interventions Since World War II* (Monroe, ME: Common Courage Press, 2004), ISBN 9781567512526.

29 TIME, "AG Jeff Sessions Cites the Bible to Defend Separating Immigrant Families," YouTube video, 1:44, June 14, 2018, https://www.youtube.com/watch?v=P-hV67w6oYA

Chapter 5: Religious Abuse

30 This is the true story of Juliana Campoverde. In 2023, we had the great honor of presenting a panel on Spiritual Violence and Religious Abuse at the Facultad Latinoamericana de Ciencias Sociales (FLASCO) in Quito, Ecuador with Juliana's mother, Elizabeth Rodriguez and Mayra Soria, the prosecutor in her case. This story is compiled entirely from new reports (mostly in Spanish), case documents, or from conversations with Elizabeth and Mayra.

For more about the case (in English) see:

> Unreal True Crime, "The Disappearance and Murder of Juliana Campoverde," October 1, 2024, https://unrealtruecrime.com/2024/10/juliana-campoverde/

In the summer of 2023, we interviewed Mayra Soria on Teología Sin Vergüenza (in Spanish). See:

> Teología Sin Vergüenza, "Temporada 6 | Episodio 3 | Mayra Soria Escobar," streamed live June 11, 2023, YouTube video, 58:10, https://www.youtube.com/watch?v=avZNlBV7CGU

31 I was horrified to learn that child sexual abuse (CSA) is so common in churches that there is an entire insurance industry set up to insulate religious institutions from being accountable to victims and their families. Often called "Sexual Misconduct and Molestation Liability" insurance, these policies protect churches, clergy, employees, and volunteers from legal defense costs, settlements, and judgments arising from alleged sexual misconduct.

32 The information for this section was compiled from information in the following sources:

Andrew S. Denney, "Child Sex Abusers in Protestant Christian Churches: An Offender Typology," CrimRxiv, October 25, 2021, https://www.crimrxiv.com/pub/p1afmq2i/release/1

Susan Raine and Stephen A. Kent, "The Grooming of Children for Sexual Abuse in Religious Settings," *Aggression and Violent Behavior* 48 (2019): 180–189, https://doi.org/10.1016/j.avb.2019.08.017

Jason D. Spraitz and Kendra N. Bowen, "Examination of a Nascent Taxonomy of Priest Sexual Grooming," *Sexual Abuse: A Journal of Research and Treatment* (2018), https://doi.org/10.1177/1079063218809095

33 Ibid.

34 I intentionally use gendered language because in Catholic churches, only men are allowed to hold clerical positions, and senior pastors of Protestant churches are still overwhelmingly male.

35 For more on this topic, see the following suggested publications:

Laura E. Anderson, *When Religion Hurts You: Healing from Religious Trauma and the Impact of High-Control Religion.* Grand Rapids, MI: Brazos Press, 2023), ISBN 9781587435805.

Linda K. Klein, *Pure: Inside the Evangelical Movement That Shamed a Generation of Young Women and How I Broke Free.* (New York: Atria Books, 2018), ISBN 9781501124822.

Kristin Kobes Du Mez, *Jesus and John Wayne: How White Evangelicals Corrupted a Faith and Fractured a Nation.* New York: Liveright, 2020.

36 Mark 12:44

37 For more on the mental health impact of "conversion therapy," see: Soulforce Institute on Spiritual Violence, Healing and Social Change, *Killing the "Sinner" Within: Spiritual Violence against LGBTQIA+ People in "Conversion Therapy"* (Soulforce Spirit Resource Library, 2023).

38 For more on this, see Alba Onofrio, *Breaking Open: Genesis 1—The Gender of God & Creation* (Soulforce Spirit Resource Library, 2017), ISBN 978-1-7361267-0-7.

Soulforce is a social justice organization working to end the religious and political oppression of LGBTQIA+ people by dismantling white Christian Supremacy and supporting healing from Spiritual Violence. Founded in 1997, we are a U.S.-based international nonprofit committed to transforming the systems and beliefs that harm our communities. We interrogate oppressive theologies related to race, gender, sexuality, and colonialism, and offer liberatory alternatives created by and for our communities.

We confront white Christian Supremacy by naming and challenging the harm done in the name of Christianity, while nurturing spiritual healing and fortification. Our work focuses on capacity building for social justice organizations, mental health providers, and faith communities, alongside narrative change and the cultivation of spiritual imagination.

Our work builds social consciousness through politicized theological education and fosters spiritual resilience across movements. By reclaiming moral authority and centering marginalized experiences, we cultivate collective healing and strengthen efforts to advance justice for all.

Soulforce provides free downloadable educational booklets through our online Spirit Resource Library. These resources offer accessible, spiritually grounded political and theological education that centers justice for marginalized people. Designed to demystify and challenge fundamentalist ideologies, these texts invite new ways of engaging with the Bible and Christian theology. Find us online to discover how theological education can heal and empower!

www.soulforce.org

www.ingramcontent.com/pod-product-compliance
Lightning Source LLC
La Vergne TN
LVHW010614100826
845148LV00014B/2971

* 9 7 8 1 7 3 6 1 2 6 7 8 3 *